HOPE, BUT DEMAND JUSTICE

HOPE, BUT DEMAND JUSTICE
collected writings

Pat Hynes

with a foreword by
Randy Kehler

Haley's
Athol, Massachusetts

Haley's • 488 South Main Street • Athol, MA 01331
haley.antique@verizon.net • 978.249.9400

Photos from the collection of H. Patricia Hynes.
Cover wall hanging by Lesyslie Rackard.
Copy edited by Ellen Woodbury.
Proof read by Phillis Scott.

Special thanks to the late Frances Crowe for co-writing articles beginning on pages 99 and 115, to Richie Davis for writing the article beginning on page 77, and to Doug Renick for co-writing the article beginning on page 170.

With gratitude, Haley's acknowledges the following print and online publications for granting permission to reprint articles in *HOPE, BUT DEMAND JUSTICE*: *Berkshire Eagle*, *Brattleboro Reformer*, *Daily Hampshire Gazette*, *Greenfield Recorder*, Indypendent, *Informed Comment*, *Montague Reporter*, Portside, Truthdig, Truthout, the publication of the US Fish and Wildlife Service, Women's International League for Peace and Freedom, and Znet.

Library of Congress Cataloging-in-Publication Data
Names: Hynes, H. Patricia, author.
Title: Hope, but demand justice : collected writings / Pat Hynes ; with a
    foreword by Randy Kehler.
Description: Athol, Massachusetts : Haley's, 2022. | Includes
    bibliographical references. | Summary: "Pat Hynes presents her
    publications while director of Traprock Center for Peace and Justice as
    she advocates for justice, peace, and an end to war"-- Provided by
    publisher.
Identifiers: LCCN 2022001919 (print) | LCCN 2022001920 (ebook) | ISBN
    9781948380553 (paperback) | ISBN 9781948380560 (hardcover) | ISBN
    9781948380577 (pdf)
Subjects: LCSH: Social justice. | Equality. | War--Prevention. | Peace.
Classification: LCC HM671 .H96 2022 (print) | LCC HM671 (ebook) |
DDC
    303.3/72--dc23/eng/20220216
LC record available at https://lccn.loc.gov/2022001919
LC ebook record available at https://lccn.loc.gov/2022001920

For Jan,
my life partner and lodestar on our long journey together,
you have my immeasurable love and gratitude

Contents

Photos and Graphs

Why Do I Trust Pat Hynes?
a foreword by Randy Kehler

I often find when a so-called controversial subject is raised, especially when it involves policy, action, or inaction on the part of governmental bodies or elected leaders, some skeptical if not bewildered person exclaims, "Yes, but how do you know that's what's really going on?" And almost as frequently, "And whose information can we trust anyway?"

When it comes to what is actually going on in the world, I, for one, completely trust the author of *HOPE, BUT DEMAND JUSTICE*, my good friend Pat Hynes, whose guest editorials have frequently appeared in our prize-winning local newspaper, the *Greenfield Recorder*, as well as other regional newspapers and progressive online national publications.

Why do I trust Pat Hynes? First of all, I never have any doubt that she really knows what she is writing about: it's clear from her sources that she has done the research. A trained environmental engineer and former Boston University professor of environmental health, she knows what constitutes reliable research, hers as well as others'.

I know Pat well enough to know she is a strong, confident, and wise woman unafraid of being challenged or criticized, which on occasion she is. But she always responds respectfully to her critics, including those with whom she strongly disagrees.

Her understanding of the wide range of issues covered in *HOPE, BUT DEMAND JUSTICE* is guided not only by her scientific expertise and training as a researcher but also, and very importantly, by compassionate intelligence. Her empathic intelligence shines through whether the subject she writes about concerns the plight of violence-and poverty-battered families fleeing across national borders (including ours) or the unbelievably wasteful and extravagant use by the US government of its citizens' tax dollars for weapons and war or the plight of fire-ravaged forests and communities due to runaway global warming or the deep physical and psychological/moral scars suffered by military veterans of the US and other countries or the fate of women and girls everywhere who, she makes clear, always bear the heaviest brunt of poverty, violence, food scarcity, and sexual exploitation.

But, lest you think you'll come away from reading these essays feeling numb, hopeless, and depressed, please don't worry. Despite the gravity of problems she analyzes, there is a clear stream of hopefulness running through all of her essays as she describes positive, real-time actions, initiatives, and actual accomplishments on the part of ordinary citizens and a few—though still too few—enlightened elected leaders worldwide.

Be sure to read her spirit-uplifting final essay, "Hope."

I can't help but mention that Pat is one of the very few genuine experts I know who is not afraid to live out the values and ethical concerns that anchor her essays, to take a public stand on behalf of what she believes in and writes about. For example, she can often be found on the Greenfield Common during a vigil in support of nuclear disarmament or the human rights of women and girls. And as a board member and former director of Traprock Center for Peace and Justice, she helps promote the annual Peacemaker Awards made by the Center and Interfaith Council to local high school students. She recently moderated a community discussion of nonviolent community-based alternatives to traditional policing.

And I should add that I regard Pat Hynes as an excellent writer whose crisp, clear use of the English language is a joy to read. In short, the essays that follow are well worth reading ... and thinking about.

The refusal of Randy Kehler and his wife, Betsy Corner, since 1977 to pay taxes for military expenditures resulted in the 1989 ederal seizure and eventual legal forfeiture of their house in Colrain, Massachusetts, detailed in the 1997 Academy-Award-nominated documentary, *Act of Conscience.*

In the 1980s, Kehler served as executive director of the National Nuclear Weapons Freeze Campaign. He served twenty-two months in jail in the 1960s for refusing induction into the United States war in Vietnam.

He is a co-founder of the Traprock Center for Peace and Justice.

Work for Something Because It Is Good

an introduction by Pat Hynes

HOPE, BUT DEMAND JUSTICE collects articles published between 2010 and 2021 and charts a quest for peace and justice for all on our planet—humans and the web of life, some 3.5 billion years old, where we live. I conceived the articles in a time of deepened social and economic inequalities and expanding weapons budgets, as the Earth reached tipping points—points of no return—from existential climate crisis and species extinction. Many writings focus on both the evidence and obstacles that obstruct our quest for peace, justice, and a sustainable Earth with equal emphasis on policy and activism to re-right our path.

I learned in my early work as an environmental engineer responsible for Superfund-site cleanups and later as professor and co-director of many complex urban environmental justice projects that the fuller our understanding of a problem, the more likely a sustainable solution. Fuller understanding must include the human and social intelligence needed to collaborate respectfully with others, no matter our differences, so that the arc of our solutions bends toward justice.

The articles include many of our crucial local, national, and international issues. Among them:

+ nuclear power and weapons
+ climate and biodiversity crises
+ COVID-19 pandemic
+ militarism and war
+ veterans

- the possibilities of peace
- international collaborations, and
- pursuit of sexual, racial, and economic justice

Though HOPE, BUT DEMAND JUSTICE separates chapters by topic, I did not conceive of them in silos. Rather, they reside in the web of interrelated politics, the environment, economics, and all manifestations of political and social justice and injustice—the dimensioned world in which we live our lives.

I keep the following words of Vaclav Havel, playwright, dissident, and first president of the Czech Republic, nearby as a realistic beacon for living with hope in the midst of assaults on peace, on justice for all, on democracy, and on the planet that sustains our life:

> The more unpromising the situation in which we demonstrate hope, the deeper that hope is. Hope . . . is not the same as joy that things are going well . . . or . . . headed for early success, but rather an ability to work for something *because it is good.*

Those who work for good to save public forests or to save the lives of COVID patients and those who speak out against the futility of war, strive to create a future of equality for girls and women and people of color, labor to eliminate nuclear weapons—present a lifeline through HOPE, BUT DEMAND JUSTICE, which culminates in the final article, "Hope."

Everyone who cares deeply about our country and our world has advice for President Joe Biden. And here is mine.

Sustain the child security payments of the 2021 American Rescue Plan to lift millions of children out of poverty permanently.

Eliminate the Republican obstacles, spreading like toxic, invasive weeds all over the country, to limit Black voting. Republican suppression of voting rights is a coup in slow motion. Fight like a bulldog for the voting rights act, the For the People Act.

Bring back fairer taxation policy on the wealthy and corporations to reduce extreme economic inequality and its shattering consequences. Fifty-five large corporations that paid no federal income tax in 2020 spent almost $450 million together in lobbying and campaign contributions over the past three election cycles. Legal loopholes, rebates, and 2017 Republican tax cuts explain their zero federal income tax. During the pandemic, the CEO-to-worker pay gap widened at top corporations, with chief executive pay rising to unprecedented levels. Many Americans are losing financially while big corporations and the wealthy are winning. Smells like plutocracy, not democracy.

Restrict the omnipotent right to guns and guarantee the human rights to housing, healthcare, and a healthful environment.

Create a US Department of Peace and *reduce the military budget substantially*. Warring tribes of the Iroquois buried their weapons and have enjoyed peace as the Iroquois Confederacy for more than three hundred years. Little more than seventy-five years ago, European nations were engaged in a bloodbath. In 2012, the European Union was awarded the Nobel Peace Prize for transforming "Europe from a continent of war to a continent of peace." Why not take the high road and aspire to this model of union at peace globally?

Bring the same effort you prize in talking with the other side, in-house—the increasingly conservative and intransigent Republican Party—to international politics and *end the belligerent, militaristic posturing* toward Russia and China. Bringing the US into a multilateral world will bring our country back better and could lead us toward an era of negotiated peace. That would guarantee authentic national security more reliably than a trillion-dollar defense and security budget.

Getting over being top cop in the world could pave the way to eliminating nuclear weapons. Which would you rather have as your legacy: ridding the world of nuclear weapons or augmenting the greatest immediate threat to life on earth, which is the current course you are on?

Turn your words of elevating diplomacy as our tool of first resort into deeds. Drop the murderous sanctions against Venezuela—that suffering country is hardly a national security threat—and renew our agreement with Iran on mutual terms. Establish a neighbor-to-neighbor relationship with Cuba—neither a threat nor an enemy but only a small socialist alternative to capitalism—to address our common interests.

Have you considered that our society's epidemic in mass murders with military-style weapons and militarized police is the homeland replication of our vaunted global military supremacy and war without end? We Americans live in a continuum of violence. Consider this: the US and allies have dropped more than 326,000 bombs and missiles on other countries since 2001. 2020 was the deadliest for gun violence in our country in twenty years.

Are you proud to have your country be the top weapons merchant—top *merchant of death*—in the world for a recent twenty-eight of thirty years?

Why are four times as many soldiers and vets dying of suicide than in combat? Could it be the lack of meaning and just cause in our wars?

Recover your early promises to refugees at our border with Mexico, promises abandoned as your administration keeps immigrant children and adults incarcerated, turns away children and adult asylum seekers to refugee tent camps in Mexico, and tells Guatemalans, *"Do not come."*

Stand by your commitment to reduce carbon emissions in half from 2005 emissions by 2030 and to net zero by 2050 no matter the pressure from fossil fuel, biomass, and nuclear lobbies. Drop subsidies to those polluting industries. The record heat, fires, and floods of summer 2021 instruct: *Build Back Better=Build Back with Renewables and Efficiency* through your American Jobs Plan.

Worried about Social Security fund staying solvent? Here's one solution: raise the income cap on Social Security, which is currently $142,800.

Replace the engine of endless growth with one that respects the limits of our biosphere. Humans had already surpassed the limit at our peril by 170% in 2021. We must solve climate and nature together—they are inseparable crises.

Heed your spiritual mentor Pope Francis: *"We need to slow down, take stock, and design better ways of living together on this earth."*

We Need Every Part of the Thread

The Earth is a relative, not a commodity.

—Leah Penniman

A thread joining personal and community activism to crucial government and economy reform courses through consideration of the environment. All are needed to sustain life on our already diminished primal home—our planet Earth.

Earth Day 1970, still the largest citizen demonstration in US history, was catalyzed in large part by the political inspiration of one woman and one book, Rachel Carson's *Silent Spring* published in 1962. So also were the creation of the US Environmental Protection Agency, EPA, in 1970 and a litany of environmental legislation passed in that decade. Her book was translated almost immediately into some thirty languages; swiftly, the environmental movement and legislation grew to encompass the entire industrial world.

In early 2007, I was asked by the US Fish and Wildlife Service to contribute to a blog the agency created to honor the legacy of Carson, who had worked there for fifteen years as a marine biologist and then editor in the 1940s and early 1950s. I chose a collection of her lesser-known writings, letters, and speeches, *Lost Woods*, to explore what kindled the fire of her passion—her *"superpower"*—for the Earth. That same searing power sustained her later in facing immense pesticide industry backlash against *Silent Spring*, including misogynist taunts of her as a "spinster" writing about genetics, as a "nun of nature" hardly a serious scientist, and more. An entry from the blog is included here.

Yet, as much as the United States progressed in the 1970s with the creation of the EPA and Congress enacting a tsunami of landmark environmental legislation that established significant controls on industrial pollution of air, water, and soil, another fate of the Earth issue emerged. The climate crisis began to manifest, undetected by most in the seventies *with the exception of the fossil fuel industry*. In that decade, Exxon Corporation scientists privately warned the company about climate warming from fossil fuel use, but the company stifled the information.

Early corporate deception by Exxon coupled with oil industry-funded think tanks and the massive fossil fuels lobby, implanted and fostered denial of climate change for more than four decades up to and through the Trump administration. Consequently, the federal government justified low investment in renewable energy. That industry/government cabal has led us to where we are today: at the cliff edge of irreversible climate and biodiversity tipping points, as the following review of *Burning Up* lays bare. The fracking industry, promoted by the Trump and Obama administrations and riddled with corruption, adds the powerful greenhouse gas methane to an already overheating atmosphere, as chronicled in the following book review of *Frackopoly*.

The corporate capitalist economy is embedded in nature as it extracts minerals and fossil fuels, depletes marine life and soil, and harvests plant life at such a rate that we need the equivalent of 1.56 Earths to sustain this plunder. In other words, we are living beyond nature's means to sustain us. But who are the "we"?

The wealthiest ten percent of humanity is responsible for fifty percent of the planet's consumption-based fossil fuel emissions, while the poorest half of humankind contributes only ten percent. Yet, who pays the price of climate disruption with their lives and livelihoods? Those least responsible, the poorest and most vulnerable to climate crises—a profound environmental injustice. Within a few decades, up to a billion of those least liable for extreme droughts, wildfires, floods, marine pollution, and rising seas could be climate refugees.

We need every part of the thread at work from immense citizen action, especially the passionate upwelling of youth environmental groups across the world, to a government-created Green New Deal. Crucially, we need to reduce the supersized military budget and reframe "national security" from a militarist mindset of "enemies" to one of multilateral partnerships. We need radical reform of capitalism to convert our economic model and structure from plundering the planet into a partner equally committed to democracy and sustainability of life on our planet. *Earth is a relative, not a commodity.*

We need all of those if we are to spare our world, our global home and family, from the worst of climate and biodiversity crises. *Any environmental action we take now is worth one hundred of the same a decade from now.*

We Loved Our Trees and Waters

One recent summer, I saw a young man standing by a large dusty gray turtle on the Turners Falls bike path, shielding this fellow creature from oncoming bikers. I recalled the Native American poet Joy Harjo's words I had read that morning:

> . . . *We loved our trees and waters*
>
> *And the creatures and earth and skies*
>
> *In that beloved place,*
>
> *Those beings were our companions*
>
> *Even as they fed us, cared for us . . .*

I remembered, too, my neighbor Sally Pick's sheer joy showing me the container in which she was raising endangered Monarch butterflies from larvae and caterpillars, which she would release when mature for their two-thousand-mile journey to Mexico. And I thought of my brother Ed, a prize-winning organic gardener in Lewes, Delaware, who sent his sisters milkweed seeds to plant for the Monarch.

How many of us, myself included, knowing of immense insect losses in recent years, carry spiders and other insects to the door, rather than crush them in our homes?

In the early twentieth century, the crisis of plant and animal extinction has hurtled into the foreground after decades of human disregard, inspiring a torrent of actions and activism. Pollinator gardens are emerging all over western Massachusetts. Recently,

Greening Greenfield, with the Traprock Center for Peace and Justice as co-sponsor, offered the forum *Pollinators! Silent Spring and Rachel Carson's Legacy* to launch a season of education about pollinator gardens and planting in Greenfield.

In 2019, the Wendell State Forest Alliance arose to oppose logging for profit on eighty acres of an old oak stand in Wendell State Forest, using nonviolent tactics to block equipment from entry into the forest and also appealing in district court to stop the logging. Though unsuccessful, they remain undeterred, championing House Bill 897, An Act Relative to Forest Protection. That 2020 legislation would designate state-owned land, comprising twenty percent of forested land in Massachusetts, as parks for recreation and reserves where ecosystems are conserved.

Why?

Older trees remove and sequester more global-warming carbon dioxide than younger trees. Re-planted logged areas take decades to replace the efficient carbon capture of mature trees. Forests hold moisture in their soil, thereby diminishing runoff and soil loss and, thus, replenishing groundwater. They support whole ecosystems of plants and animals lost when logged. Given extreme rates of extinction of insects, other animals, and plants, we cannot risk losing the ecosystems in mature forests to logging for profit-making— forests with the most endangered plants and animals, according to climate scientist William Moomaw—only to wait decades for new forests to replace lost ones.

How critical is the ongoing loss of animals and plants? The loss of three billion birds during the past fifty years in North America, as columnist Bill Danielson of *The Recorder* of Greenfield lamented in a recent column, is the just the tip of the iceberg. We are in a new period of extinction—a thousand times the rate of extinction before humans existed—called the Sixth Extinction, the first extinction caused by human activity.

Up to sixty percent of mammals, birds, fish, reptiles, and amphibians have disappeared since the 1970s. More than forty percent of insect species are threatened with extinction, many of them food pollinators. The once-rich ecosystem of coral reefs is home to more than a quarter of all marine species: twenty-five percent of coral reefs are virtually dead and the remaining almost surely endangered in the near future.

The primary causes of our planet's ecosystem collapse are well established:

+ global use of pesticides; burning of rainforest for cattle ranching
+ logging of forests, including biodiversity-rich US southeastern forests, for highly polluting industrial wood burning plants here and in Europe, and
+ the climate crisis

Journalist Dahr Jamail contrasted our Western culture with that of Indigenous cultures, after interviewing climate scientists and biologists across the world on the fate of the planet given the accelerating pace of loss of plants, animals, and glaciers; climate warming; and sea-level rise. He writes, "While Western . . . culture believes in rights, Indigenous cultures teach us of obligations that we are born into: obligations to those who came before, to those who will come after, and to the Earth itself. When we orient ourselves around the question "What are our obligations?" the deeper question immediately arises: 'From this moment on, knowing what is happening to the planet, to what do we devote our life?'"

All of us—parents, grandparents, aunts and uncles, librarians, teachers and mentors of youth, journalists, land users and landowners, and politicians—have a critical responsibility to honor our obligations to nature and to share the knowledge with children. Nature makes our life possible. Living with such awareness, Native Americans address the Earth as our sacred Mother. Without her web/womb of life we humans would not continue to exist as a species.

Let us spend time in nature, restore our sense of wonder in nature, and support a lifelong love of and responsibility for the natural world in our children.

Originally published October 31, 2019 as guest editorial in the *Montague Reporter*. Reprinted with permission.

Civil Disobedience in the
Time of Climate Crisis

A Massachusetts judge found thirteen protestors who obstructed construction of a high-pressure fracked gas pipeline in West Roxbury, Massachusetts, not responsible on March 27, 2018 for charges of trespassing and disturbing the peace. The judge ruled that the potential environmental and public health impacts of the pipeline—including the risk of climate change—had authorized civil disobedience as defined by law.

A Portland, Oregon, jury refused on February 27, 2020 to convict the self-identified Zenith Five—activists fighting for a "habitable future"—of blockading a train track used by Zenith Energy Corporation to transport crude oil. Their blockade consisted of building a garden over the rail line, thus making it impassable for the transport train. Their defense: they were justified in breaking the law on behalf of the planetary climate crisis. Five of six jurors voted to acquit them.

The next day, sixteen members of the Wendell State Forest Alliance and supporters gathered in Orange, Massachusetts, Municipal Court for closing arguments on why their trespassing to prevent state-supported logging in Wendell forest was necessary and justifiable. The judge had not yet rendered his decision. "Social change happens by people who . . . make sacrifices to bring critical issues to the attention of a larger public," explained their lawyer, Luke Ryan.

Thanks to citizens who practiced civil disobedience throughout the past 250 years, we are not only an independent country but also a more democratic, inclusive, and moral country.

Think of the Boston Tea Party: colonists dumped 342 chests of tea belonging to the British East India Company into Boston Harbor on December 16, 1773 to protest a British tax—*taxation without representation*—and monopoly on tea. Our history books lionize their act of civil disobedience as a catalyst of the American Revolution.

Think of Henry David Thoreau of Concord, Massachusetts. He was arrested in July of 1846 for refusing to pay his taxes in protest of slavery and the US violent occupation of Mexican territory, later the state of Texas, for the sake of expanding slavery. Today Thoreau is an icon, a model of acting by one's conscience in the face of government wrongdoing and for laying an ethical foundation for civil disobedience in his pamphlet *Civil Disobedience*.

Think of Harriet Tubman. She escaped slavery and then, at extreme risk to her own life, became a conductor on the Underground Railway, leading African slaves to freedom in defiance of the Fugitive Slave Act. Today Tubman is a nationally revered symbol of living by conscience, and our country is more democratic for her actions.

Think of the suffragists. Their picketing, relentless lobbying, creative civil disobedience, and nonviolent confrontation compelled a reluctant President Woodrow Wilson to support a federal women's suffrage amendment, ratified as the Nineteenth Amendment in 1920. Their successful dissent gave half of the population of the United States freedom to vote, thus honoring the goal of equal rights for women.

Think of Rosa Parks. In Montgomery, Alabama, "the mother of the civil rights movement" was jailed in violation of the city's racial segregation laws for refusing to give her seat on a public bus to a white man. Her historic challenge to Montgomery's racist bus laws sparked the successful Montgomery bus boycott, organized by Martin Luther King Jr. When Rosa Parks died in October 2005, the US Congress honored her by having her body lie in state in the Capitol Rotunda.

Think of decades of legislative action, protest, and civil disobedience by hundreds of disability rights activists:

- in 1990, the Americans with Disabilities Act became the most sweeping disability rights legislation in American history
- with an existential sense of urgency, thousands of climate scientists are warning governments that we are doomed within decades if we do not act immediately to slow the climate crisis, and
- in October 2019, four hundred scientists stated that civil disobedience to slow the climate crisis is necessary and justified

- in the same month, eleven thousand scientists worldwide declared a climate emergency
- in November 2019, the UN reported that devastating impacts of climate crisis are imminent

We need drastic action.

Also in November 2019, scientists warned that our earth is approaching tipping points that will cause a cascade of irreversible climate changes. In fact, a tipping point was reached in 2020 in some of the Brazilian Amazon rainforest, thus turning it into savanna, a mixed woodland-grassland ecosystem characterized by the trees being sufficiently widely spaced so that the canopy does not close.

What we—citizens, corporations, courts, and government—do about the climate crisis will determine the quality of—and even the feasibility of—life on earth within the next few decades. It is a paramount ethical issue of our day, as were independence from the British Empire, abolishing slavery, winning women's right to vote, and civil rights for African Americans and the disabled. The historic protesters were judged criminals by the courts of their day. In time, they were regarded as people of conscience who held their country to a higher moral standard against unjust laws, policy, and practices—that is, their actions were justified in order to prevent greater harm.

And we are the better for it.

The selection above represents a longer version of my expert witness testimony offered in the February 28, 2020 trial in Orange, Massachusetts Court of ten Forest Protectors of the Wendell State Forest Alliance. The trial followed their arrests for trespassing in Wendell State Forest in August 2019 to prevent clear cutting, permitted by the state of Massachusetts, of hundreds of mature oak trees.

Originally published March 11, 2020 in the *Greenfield Recorder*. Reprinted with permission.

Earth Day 2016: Retrospect and Realism

In June 1969, the Cuyahoga River caught fire from floating oil and combustible debris as it wound through Cleveland, Ohio. While not the first river fire, it was the last for that and other industrial rivers.

Federal laws enacted in the early 1970s, in particular the Clean Air Act, Clean Water Act, and creation of the Environmental Protection Agency, EPA, began a more than forty-year uphill national effort to reduce intense smog and filthy rivers. New regulations required

- catalytic converters in motor vehicles
- pollution capture technologies for factory air emissions
- filter and treatment technologies for factory liquid wastes discharged into rivers, and
- more advanced municipal wastewater treatment plants for human waste and street runoff

All slowly reversed the extreme degradation of our rivers and air from unfettered industrial development.

Ten months after the Cuyahoga River fire, the first Earth Day was launched. On April 22, 1970, twenty million people took to the streets in the largest political demonstration in history to date. They walked into polluted rivers with scuba gear, demonstrated at stockholders' meetings of corporate polluters, and conducted peaceful actions in front of the federal Department of the Interior. Ten thousand public elementary, middle, and high schools, two thousand colleges and universities, and almost every community took part. The US Congress formally adjourned so that senators and representatives could attend teach-ins in their districts. That afternoon I took my twenty-five eleven-year-old students to walk along Brandywine Creek, which bisects Wilmington, Delaware. Maybe we picked up trash, maybe we just walked on the cobbly streambank—I don't remember.

The kids were mostly from the older, struggling east side of downtown Wilmington and the younger, uglier, angrier projects off Northeast Boulevard. They were second-class children in a state purported to have the highest per capita income and PhDs in the United States. Downtown Wilmington, a stone's throw from where we walked, was embellished with the Hotel DuPont and the DuPont corporate headquarters. Otherwise, it was a city of de facto segregated housing and schools. A few years earlier, the national guard had policed downtown streets, so raw and so threatening was the anger of urban African–Americans in the face of blatant, punishing racist neglect and the murder of Martin Luther King.

As I watched kids jumping from stream boulder to stream boulder, I remember asking myself, *What does this have to do with them?* What do clean streams have to do with literacy, jobs, housing, and human dignity?

Time and events would answer my question.

The 1980s ushered in EPA's Superfund and hazardous waste programs, the goals of which were to identify the most toxic of solid and liquid manufacturing waste flagrantly buried on industry sites in drums and catchall landfills leaching into groundwater and nearby water bodies or burned in open air and in unregulated incinerators.

It was in this decade that I found the answer to my question: *What does Earth Day have to do with my eleven-year-old second-class citizens?*

The Housatonic River in western Massachusetts was neither drinkable nor swimmable, and its banks hosted health-warning signs for those fishing when I was assigned in the early 1980s as an EPA environmental engineer to oversee the study of the river's pollution for eventual cleanup. General Electric Company's transformer division in Pittsfield, Massachusetts, had used the river as a sewer for its PCB-laden industrial waste, whose toxicity magnified in the river's food chain and concentrated in fish. Studies showed that the contaminated sediments carried by the river amassed behind downstream dams. The challenge of possible dredging and burying contaminated sediments in a protected site took me to meeting upon meeting with officials and townspeople of downstream towns to discuss a potential burial site for toxic sediments in their town. Predictably, no town was willing to provide a site, which eventually left one option—a landfill in Warren County, North Carolina, designated by the state and EPA for PCB wastes.

Not long after, I learned through national news of a public protest in Warren County led by African-American women who formed a human chain and blocked the entry to the landfill. Their message: stop dumping other people's industrial waste in our community.

With more than five hundred arrests, Warren County nonviolent protests and marches ignited the movement for environmental justice in the United States. This now international movement unites poor, excessively polluted communities of color and Native American lands in the US with climate-justice activists in developing countries disproportionately burdened with drought, growing deserts, food shortages, and sea-level rise from climate change primarily caused by wealthy industrial countries.

In the 1990s, new onslaughts of mal-development began in industrial agriculture. Rachel Carson's pathbreaking *Silent Spring* had exposed the "chemical rain of death" on farms, forests, and yards following World War II, thus succeeding in DDT being taken off the US market, though the government allowed it to be manufactured for sale abroad.

With regulatory focus on toxic, long-lived insecticides that accumulate up the food chain, pesticide industries turned to research and manufacturing genetically modified organisms, GMO, seeds, mainly ones that would resist the companies' herbicides. Thus, pesticide industries aimed to control global agriculture as they morphed into vertically integrated companies manufacturing genetically modified seed and herbicide companies. GMO acreage has grown exponentially worldwide—282 million acres are planted in Monsanto's GMO crops, up a hundredfold since 1996, according to Food and Water Watch, together with the use of herbicides, resulting in the vicious cycle of herbicide-resistant weeds, called superweeds, requiring greater use of herbicides.

In the twenty-first century, climate change is the defining issue of our times. *It is an issue of peace* or, more precisely, of militarism and war. Beginning with the belligerent Carter Doctrine in the late seventies in response to the Arab oil embargo, the US launched what would grow since 1991 into a total military presence in the Middle East over access to oil and US wars. The US naval presence in the Persian Gulf, with its entry and exit point at the Strait of Hormuz, had cost US taxpayers an estimated eight trillion dollars by 2010, one of the many externalized costs that subsidize fossil fuels.

Climate change accelerates the Sixth Extinction and ecological collapse together with pollution and loss of habitat. A recent study of global fisheries forecasts the population collapse by 2048 of "all fish currently caught commercially." Warming marine waters are pushing fish away from the tropics toward the poles, thus depriving poorer equatorial countries of their dominant source of protein. The changing chemistry of warming and more acidic oceans portends an unprecedented loss of the ocean's nursery and most biodiverse ecosystem on Earth—coral reefs.

Climate change is an issue of human survival. At current rates of melting, sea-level rise will reach six feet minimally by 2100, threatening fourteen hundred cities, among them New York City, San Diego, Boston, Miami, and thousands of others across the world. New research by James Hansen and colleagues forecasts a marine Armageddon: an estimated several meters of sea-level rise within this century with melting of glacial sheets in Antarctica and Greenland, thus drowning coastal cities worldwide.

Climate change is an issue of justice. "We are all on the Titanic," observed Kenyan ecologist Ruth Nyambura at the 2015 United Nations Conference on Climate Change in Paris, "but only the wealthy own the lifeboats." The developing world and the poor—those least responsible for climate change—are the most vulnerable to extremes of climate. Of the ten most affected countries between 1994 and 2014, nine were developing countries in Asia and Central America and the country of Haiti, which suffered extreme, record-breaking natural catastrophes from intense rain, flooding, mudslides, typhoons, and hurricanes.

Capitalism wedded to delusional American Manifest Destiny—including our fatuous decades-long effort to control the Middle East and recent militarized pivot to Asia—meets its limits in Nature. Either we heed those limits immediately and aggressively, or we face an ecocide from which not even those who own lifeboats will escape.

Always, indigenous peoples have grasped this. In their dramatic presence at the Paris Climate Summit, they exposed most clearly and cogently the root causes of climate change: namely, that Western science, technology, and capitalist economies regard Nature/Mother Earth as a lifeless trove of commodities—minerals, metals, coal, oil, gas, uranium, and water—to exploit ruthlessly and relentlessly for amassing wealth. Their primal message to the world is that the

Earth is our sacred source of life and that the dominant world view commodifies nature and subordinates all other rights—human rights and the rights of nature—at our peril.

Prescient children understand the threat posed by the commodification of Nature. In 2015 twenty-one young people, members of Our Children's Trust, filed a landmark climate-change lawsuit in all fifty states against the federal government on the grounds that the government's continued exploitation of fossil fuels violates the rights of the next generation to a stable climate and healthy future. Deciding in favor of the plaintiffs, Oregon's Federal District Court Judge Thomas Coffin ruled against the federal government and fossil fuel trade associations' motions to dismiss the case.

Based on the doctrine of public trust, the Children's Trust lawsuit alleges that just as the federal government must protect public waterways and seashores for public use, so also the climate and atmosphere must be protected for public well-being. The judge called the case "unprecedented," and nineteen-year-old lead plaintiff, Kelsey Juliana, said in response to the ruling: "This will be the trial of the century that will determine if we have a right to a livable future, or if corporate power will continue to deny our rights for the sake of their own wealth."

Three fossil fuel industry trade associations, which joined the government as defendants, called the case "a direct, substantial threat to [their] businesses."

Originally published April 19, 2020 at *Portside*. Reprinted with permission.

Natural Gas: A Bridge to Climate Disaster

Frackopoly: The Battle for the Future of Energy and the Environment
by Wenonah Hauter
The New Press. 2016

Branding fracked natural gas as a *bridge* fuel to renewable energy is one of the great fossil fuel ruses of our times. Two other scams include the trope that *natural gas is safe and green* and the merchandising of doubt about climate change since the 1970s. Together they are driving us down the path of destruction by fire and water (or lack thereof) with implacable wildfires, drought, deluges, warming seas, and sea-level rise.

In her latest book, *Frackopoly: The Battle for the Future of Energy and the Environment*, Wenonah Hauter gives readers a bracing critique of the practice, finance schemes, and politics of fracking as well as a thorough, up-to-the-minute account of grassroots mobilizing to oppose fracking, new oil and gas pipelines, and liquid natural gas export terminals. The energy coursing through *Frackopoly* stems from Hauter's unblinking floodlight on the coddled, corrupt, and risk-driven fracking corporations, many of them the financial progeny of the robber barons. It is a fitting companion to Naomi Orestes's and Erik Conway's acclaimed *Merchants of Doubt*. In their exposé, the authors excavate the cover-up of climate change since the 1970s by Exxon and other fossil fuel companies and the perverse Republican campaign, abetted by mainstream media, to discredit climate change, scientists, and science.

The corporate frackers' exploits are counterpoised with histories of unflinching grassroots campaigns—with some remarkable victories—to leave fossil fuels in the ground. Among them are a detailed case study of the uphill victory to ban fracking in New York State and an overview from coast to coast of the ban movement, grounded in the environmental and health harms of fracking for oil and gas. As Hauter documents, such harms include:

- immense potable water use for fracking even in regions of water scarcity
- contaminated aquifers and wells; earthquakes induced by deep injection wastewater disposal
- methane leaks at all points of production, transportation, storage and use, and
- respiratory, neurological and reproductive health impacts on nearby residents

She contrasts the tenacious fracking-ban movement in rural communities, on Native American lands, and in urban communities of color with the well-heeled mainstream environmental organizations' concession of "regulating" fracking to lessen spills, methane leaks, and drinking-water contamination. Such blinkered groups—among them the Environmental Defense Fund—play into our government's national policy of an energy buffet with renewables providing no more than between twenty and twenty-five percent. The natural gas "bridge" they champion, has been tagged a "bridge to nowhere," a "bridge over a crumbling highway," and "a bridge to climate disaster," given that new natural-gas plants and infrastructure being built for fracked gas have a forty-year lifespan. But with an annual average of 22.5 million African, Asian, Pacific Island, and indigenous Alaskan climate refugees, the world does not have forty years to spare.

Another rich seam lies in the book's documentation of the leniency of federal and state regulation on behalf of the oil and gas industries conjoined with the largesse doled out in:

+ tax breaks, loopholes, and shelters
+ federal research and development, R&D, funds, and
+ land grants and investments in ports and inland waterways

Since the 1970s, more than ten trillion gallons of wastewater from oil and gas drilling have been categorized as non-hazardous and discharged into "Class 2" injection wells. According to industry promoters and regulators interviewed by ProPublica, those wells are loosely regulated and receive less scrutiny so as to protect the oil and gas industry from costly regulation and, thus, help sustain oil and gas production.

Tax policy and subsidies made all early fossil fuel and nuclear energy transitions possible, whereas government support for emerging renewables, including research and development, pales in comparison. Further, the costs from fossil-fuel pollution, so-called externalities, which include groundwater pollution from wastewater injection wells, $7.3 trillion spent on patrolling the Persian Gulf oil shipments since the late seventies, climate change, and tens of thousands of premature deaths each year, are not borne by the industry. We citizens foot the bill.

What's especially significant in *Frackopoly*—and rare in much fracking literature—is that the author foregrounds the plague of social harms emanating from what she calls "man camps," code for oil- and gas-worker settlements. In the small town of Williston, North Dakota, for example, traffic accidents, crime, social disturbances from drunkenness and drug use, and rape have all increased significantly. Since 2000 when the town doubled in size with oil- and gas-fracking workers, a woman in Williston is more than twice as likely to be raped as in the rest of North Dakota.

With 2.5 million miles of oil and gas pipelines currently crisscrossing the country from east to west and north to south, and nineteen now-pending pipeline projects planned for the whole Appalachian Basin on the East Coast, why does Hauter envisage the hundreds of steadfast actions nationwide to stop new pipelines as a titanic challenge to both the industry and government policy? The answer is perhaps best parsed by Mark Trahant of The Standing Rock Sioux fighting the Dakota Access Pipeline of 1,172 miles being constructed from Bakken oil fields in North Dakota to oil refineries in Illinois. He points to the power of people using social media to mobilize thousands of Native and grassroots protesters, which by September 2016 included the historic support of 189 tribal governments. Protectors, as those gathered prefer to be known, have the moral high ground, he says, in their campaigns to protect their water, ancestral territories, and sacred sites. And, further, now is "The Moment" to stop pipelines and keep fossil fuels in the ground. Why now? A rising chorus of investment companies, among them the prominent global stock market index company, MSCI, are warning investors to get out of fossil fuels before they become "stranded assets" due to price volatility and competition from renewables. Moreover, portfolios that have divested from fossil fuels over the past five years are outperforming those that haven't.

Sobering analysis from the Post Carbon Institute, though, counterbalances "moment-is-now" surety. For example, oil is essential to the modern world because local, national, and global transport of goods by heavy trucks as well as airplanes and container ships carrying food, raw materials, and manufactured goods, including solar panels and wind turbine parts, rely on oil. Moreover, such means of industrial cargo transport have no current energy substitute, unlike cars and trains that can be solar-powered.

The revolution in solar and wind energy has focused largely on renewably generated electricity for domestic and commercial light, heat, and appliances while transportation consumes an estimated thirty percent of fossil fuels used in the United States. Transitioning to renewable, non-oil fuels will take two or more decades and has been "woefully insufficient" while we are rapidly running out of time to keep rising temperatures below the critical threshold of 1.5 degrees centigrade. The institute urges that, while building a renewable future, we must rapidly transition to local economies, creating resilience and capacity to produce and transport goods locally and regionally.

But the transition to local, renewably-powered towns and cities must be a *just transition* for all, guided by "principles of social justice and environmental justice," adds Dallas Goldtooth, organizer for the Indigenous Environmental Network. A society powered by solar, wind, and water will not necessarily be a just society that works to rid itself of gender, racial, and economic injustice unless it seeks to do so.

As founder and executive director of Food & Water Watch, a watchdog group with offices throughout the United States and the first national organization to support a ban on fracking, Wenonah Hauter writes from a position of expertise on government and corporate accountability as well as on-the-ground activism and advocacy.

Reading *Frackopoly* is something of a roller coaster ride generating visceral disgust with reckless corporate maneuvers and weak, enabling state and federal regulators in tandem with exultation over grassroots victories, numbering more than five hundred in communities that have passed measures to stop fracking. There is not one expendable sentence in the book. It should be read side-by-side with the ominous analysis of the Post Carbon Institute and also Gretchen Bakke's book, *The Grid*, where she contends that the national electrical grid is the "weakest link" in reaching our goal of one hundred percent renewable power.

Originally published November 12, 2016 at *Truthdig*. Reprinted with permission.

Madness Driving Climate Catastrophe

Burning Up: A Global History of Fossil Fuel Consumption
by Simon Pirani
Pluto Press. 2018

The Great Acceleration is the designation given to the past seventy years during which industrial countries and a handful of newly rich developing countries extracted and consumed fossil fuels at a reckless rate. While accurate, the metaphor might suggest progress rather than ominous ensuing atmospheric, terrestrial, and oceanic climate trends.

The twenty hottest years on record have occurred since 1995 almost in tandem with impotent United Nations climate negotiations begun in Rio de Janeiro in 1992 and followed by the Kyoto Protocol in 1997 and conferences in Copenhagen in 2009, Paris in 2015, and Poland in 2018. Yet, even with near global consensus on the necessity to reduce climate-warming emissions radically by 2030 and non-binding national pledges to do so, carbon dioxide—CO_2—emissions rose by 2.7 percent in 2018 and 0.6% in 2019. CO_2 concentrations in the atmosphere have risen unremittingly to levels not prevailing since hundreds of thousands of and possibly more than six million years ago.

Historian and energy researcher Simon Pirani likens the collective failure to act on climate change to what he calls the "collective madness" of World War I, whence, he writes, old world imperial loyalties set loose the juggernaut of a mindless, pointless bloodbath of Europe's boys and young men that ended only from morbid exhaustion on all sides. In *Burning Up: A Global History of Fossil Fuel Consumption*, Pirani sets out to plumb the political, social, and economic causes of the "madness that is producing global warming." His is a critically needed departure from much climate-crisis writing and activism that focuses solely on technology, individual consumption, and population growth as drivers of climate change.

Burning Up takes a structural and a muscular evidence-based tack, and in doing shows us the dominant *axis of evil* driving climate change. For example, though individuals are consumers of fossil fuel for electricity, heat, air conditioning, goods, and services, the author contends, "they do so in the context of social and economic systems over which they may have little control."

Corporate wealth-seeking and power over the political elite drive the economy and determine the modes of technology, production and consumption, namely fossil fuels, for electricity, heating, cooling and commercial products like cement, steel, plastics, according to Pirani, and as fuel for transportation and road-building, construction, and the military. The same corporate power grifters promote mass consumption through marketing, he writes, with *hidden persuaders*, and encode fossil fuel dependence through promoting car-oriented development globally.

A handful of large rich countries and some wealthier developing countries are included in the book, with the United States as central actor and agent for more reasons than its historical mega consumption of fossil fuels. The US has functioned as the stimulant and model for social, economic, and political systems driving growth of gross domestic product in other rich and newly rich countries and resulting in fossil fuel use spiraling "out of control since mid twentieth century." Further, the US mode of consumption is continually being reproduced across the world. Pirani's temporal focus is from the 1950s to the present, coinciding with the postwar "great acceleration," in which the impact of technology and economies on nature has been swift and drastic.

Among his most cogent examples of the political and economic elite driving climate change is the calculated design, now replicated throughout the world, of cities for the car. Car-centered transport in the United States between World War I and World War II "became a template for the world and shaped fossil fuel consumption patterns internationally." Industry consolidated from eighty-eight carmakers in 1921 to ten in 1935, with the big three—Ford, GM, and Chrysler—encompassing ninety percent of the market and ranking among the most powerful corporate lobbies in the world. In the US, they bought up and shut down trolley systems and helped displace railways with road transport for buses, trucks, and cars.

The auto industry thus stimulated car-centered urban design and urban renewal in the case of older cities and was embedded in the post-fifties mushrooming of car-oriented suburbs. Government invested in building fossil fuel-intensive roads and highways through cities, manufacturers designed cars for obsolescence, and industry pioneered the annual style change in cars. All were the result of "corporate strategies to stimulate consumer demand," even during the Depression.

As for the future, fifty-five percent of the world's people now inhabit cities with a projected increase to sixty-eight percent by 2050. Car-based urbanization drives consumption of fossil fuels, especially because cities are not designed centrally for public transportation. And, as Pirani underscores, governments, developers, and corporate interests, not the individuals who live in them, shape the design of cities and constrain individual choice. Federal tax policy and subsidies enabled all early fossil fuel and nuclear energy transitions, whereas government support for emerging renewables pales in comparison, a global phenomenon, as Pirani's comparative data substantiates.

In the United States, opponents of renewable technologies, promoters of fossil fuels and nuclear power, and diehard critics of government subsidies to renewable technologies have branded federal energy subsidies as an unfair handout to the solar and wind sector—a welfare program, in their view, giving advantage to the renewables industry that would collapse if it had to compete with coal, oil, gas, and nuclear.

However, a historical study of government subsidies to all energy technologies, not included in *Burning Up*, easily trounces the myth that renewables would collapse without subsidies. Federal incentives for the first fifteen years of subsidy life were five times greater for oil and gas and ten times greater for nuclear power than for emerging renewable technologies. Indirect government support for wood and fossil fuels includes land grants for early timber stands and railroads for coal and other fuels. Early government-supported research and development for non-renewable energy industries was significantly greater than for renewables and efficiency. Moreover, there is no counterpart in renewable energy subsidies to the $7.3 trillion spent by the US Department of Defense from 1976 through 2007 patrolling the Persian Gulf to protect US oil shipments.

Finally, as many researchers pre-dating Pirani have attested, the fossil fuel and nuclear power industries are not held financially liable for premature deaths and morbidity from air pollution from fossil fuel combustion nor for the costs of ultimate disposal of nuclear waste. Nor do fossil fuel industries pay their fair share for their role in the record loss of species and coral reefs, five-fold increase in natural disasters since 1970, and property damage due to global warming emissions.

Pirani's closing chapters reinforce his opening message. Corporate capitalism and political elites have led us, by their dominant choice of fossil-fuel-based energy and technology, to the point of "burning up." Given they are leading the human race and much other life to extinction, he urges us to take the road less travelled: " . . . [T]he decisive actor [must be] society—all of it collectively—rather than political elites."

I am reminded of the precocious Greta Thunberg, the then fifteen-year-old Swedish climate activist, speaking at the UN climate conference in 2018 on behalf of the global youth climate movement. Every day the world uses some hundred million barrels of oil, yet "there are no politics to change that, no politics to keep the oil in the ground," she said. "Since our leaders are behaving like children, we will have to take the responsibility they should have taken long ago. There is no time to continue down this road of madness. We have come to let them know that change is coming whether they like it or not. The people will rise to the challenge."

Since Greta Thunberg's speech, tens of thousands of young students across the world are following her example, going on strike from school one day a week to pressure their governments to abide by their commitments to reduce climate change emissions.

Pirani concludes with steps for "breaking the resistance of incumbent interests" that are disappointingly general and, thus, not quickly actionable. In the spirit of his conclusion, I would point to a few recent standouts of taking action and taking back our future:

+ the pragmatic and progressive Green New Deal
+ the meteoric rise of young political action groups like the Sunrise Movement in the US, and

- the infectious youth climate action lawsuit Juliana v. US, filed by children and young adults against the US government for failing to limit the effects of climate change on human health

May we be spared the time needed—given the rapidity of climate breakdown—to disrupt the hold of corporate wealth and power and to implement the Green New Deal through a publicly owned Green Tennessee Valley Authority.

Originally published April 5, 2019 at *Truthdig*. Reprinted with permission.

War and the True Tragedy of the Commons

"A world that wants to make peace with the environment cannot continue to fight wars or to sacrifice human health and the earth's ecosystems preparing for them."

—Michael Renner

War and Public Health

"Tragedy of the Commons," Garrett Hardin's 1968 polarizing essay published in *Science*, essentially targeted overpopulation—read poor women—as the prime threat to sustainable life on our finite planet Earth. Hardin and many who consumed his thesis failed to single out the very small but politically powerful population responsible for immense environmental impact—the military complex. Per capita, the military with its national security and intelligence advisors, civilian defense contractors, and elites of government—read powerful men and a few women—is the most polluting human population. Their well-glued solidarity has cloaked their extraordinary debt of pollution, destruction of land, and use of finite resources in the paternalistic mantle of national security.

Since the origins of recorded history, war chroniclers have told of tactical environmental destruction:
- destroying crops, forest, and infrastructure
- polluting water supply and breaching dikes to flood enemy troops and fields; salting enemies' fields, and
- catapulting infected blankets into enemy garrisons and so on

During the American Civil War, a handful of Confederates attempted to burn down New York City and plotted both to poison the city's drinking-water-supply reservoir and to spread yellow fever throughout Washington, DC. The Chinese government committed perhaps the single most destructive wartime act in history during Japan's 1937-1945 war against China. To deter the Japanese advance, the Chinese dynamited a dike near Chengchow, releasing impounded Yellow River water. Not only did the floodwaters drown the several thousand advancing Japanese soldiers, they also destroyed four thousand villages, eleven cities, and several million hectares of farmland and killed several hundred thousand Chinese civilians.

War breeds environmental destruction, and just as war victims and war tactics have changed in recent times, so also has the scale of environmental destruction from war. The casualties of war in the late twentieth and early twenty-first centuries have shifted from combatant soldiers to innocent civilians, with an estimated nine civilian deaths for every soldier death. The locus of war has moved from battlefields to urban and rural population centers, causing massive numbers of residents to flee and imminent health crises of contaminated water, poor sanitation, inadequate health care, malnourishment, overcrowding, and sexual predation in refugee camps. By 2011 nearly half of the world's refugees—4.73 million Afghanis and Iraqis—were fleeing US-led wars and ensuing civil conflicts in their countries.

Widespread conflict in populated rural areas jeopardizes vital public health campaigns. The North-South Sudanese conflict threatened the village-based public health campaign to eliminate the human parasite, guinea worm, because war and neglect had made South Sudan the worm's last stronghold. All the villages where people caught guinea worm in 2010 were suffering armed conflicts; public health campaign staff and residents had fled the fighting. With the conflict ending, the government hoped to eradicate guinea worm—"the peace dividend we can give the world," said the health minister responsible for the eradication program.

Likewise, modern war and militarism have a staggering impact on nature and our lived environment—by:

- the kinds of weapons used, including long-lived concealed explosives, toxic chemicals, and radiation
- the "shock and awe" intensity of industrial warfare, and

+ the massive exploitation of natural resources and fossil fuels to support militarism

By 1990, researchers had estimated that the world's military accounted for from five to ten percent of global air pollution, including carbon dioxide, ozone-depletion, smog, and acid-forming chemicals. The Research Institute for Peace Policy in Starnberg, Germany, calculated that twenty percent of all global environmental degradation was due to military and related activities.

Larger, more powerful weapons systems, naval ships, and fighter planes usurp and contaminate huge swaths of land, habitat, groundwater, and soil. A World War II fighter plane "required a maneuvering radius of about 9 kilometers, compared with 75 kilometers in 1990 and a projected 150-185 kilometers for the next generation of jets." The amount of land and airspace mandated by armed forces for war games, including bombing and shooting ranges, has increased by at least 20 times since World War II. Up to half of US airspace is used for military purposes. Millions of acres of US territory are consigned to military use, resulting in "a scorched-earth policy against an imaginary foe."

As for scorched earth against real "foes," one Vietnam veteran described the rain of death in the Vietnam War—with bombs, mortars, napalm, and other chemical warfare pouring out of the sky—as a war against the environment creating twenty million bomb craters and "reducing the Earth to ashes." During the 1991 Gulf War, the deliberate release by Iraq of an estimated sixty million barrels of Kuwaiti oil from torched wells, storage tanks, and pipelines, killed thousands of migratory and marine wildlife, contaminated groundwater and offshore Kuwaiti waters and marine habitats, and left a heavy, long-lasting shroud of soot and combustion gases particularly injurious to those with respiratory illness and ailments.

Ecologists have concluded that fragile desert environments may take much longer than other hardier environments to recover— decades to hundreds or even a thousand years—from both soot and oil droplets of the Gulf War oil fires that damaged desert vegetation and rangelands. An even greater impact may be the physical damage of military tanks, trucks, and other heavy vehicles crisscrossing the fragile desert, crushing the millimeter-thin layer of microorganisms that forms a crust at the top of the soil, protecting it from erosion, and resulting in increased sandstorms and moving dunes.

War between nations has intensified militarily and, thus, magnified natural resource exploitation and ecological devastation. In the early 1980s, the Center for Disarmament estimated that global military operations used more aluminum, copper, nickel, and platinum than the entire Third World did for development. US military use of various metals ranges from five to forty percent of civilian use. During the six-week air war during the 1991 Gulf War and the hundred-hour ground war, "more weapons were reportedly used than during the protracted Vietnam War."

By US Army estimates, the first three weeks of the 2003 war in Iraq consumed forty million gallons of fuel, an amount equivalent to what eighty thousand Americans would use for a year's worth of driving. In the same war, the United States employed more than twenty weapons systems that contain depleted uranium, in amounts weighing from three hundred grams to seven tons. Some estimate that more than a thousand tons of depleted uranium were deployed, although the Pentagon is tight-lipped about amounts of DU used in recent wars.

The environment has been described as "the silent casualty" of war—one could also call it "the invisible casualty" of war. Governments at war honor the fallen and give lip service to the so-called collateral damage of civilians injured and killed while they treat military pollution as the necessary cost of waging war and disdain any responsibility for remediating environmental contamination. As the muscled-up Pentagon sees it, environmental-protection laws hamstring their military training and war readiness and, thus, jeopardize national security. In retort, Karen Wayland, legislative director of the Natural Resources Defense Council, turned the military's "necessity for national defense" argument on its head: "the Pentagon's push for blanket exemptions from federal health and pollution cleanup safeguards makes a mockery of national defense. Using national security to sacrifice our nation's environmental security will endanger our health, leaving us less safe."

If, as many contend, the principal threat to world security in the twenty-first century is environmental degradation through climate change, pollution, soil erosion, habitat loss, and species extinction, then environmental destruction of war together with the massive exploitation of oil and metal resources for the military-industrial war machine, must become paramount in the work for peace. The US military is a power without precedent or competitor. The Pentagon maintains nearly a thousand military bases worldwide, and its core budget equals that of the rest of the world's military combined. Thus, documented environmental hazards of grievously polluted US military sites as well as from US-led wars and war-related activities serve as the worst-case example of global military pollution—the true *tragedy of our commons*.

Originally published August 4, 2011 at *Truthout*. Reprinted with permission.

How the Light Gets In

Every now and then I re-visit these lines of the Canadian poet and songwriter, Leonard Cohen:

> Ring the bells that cannot ring,
> Forget your perfect offering.
> There is a crack in everything.
> That's how the light gets in.

In times of climate change denial, macho military chest-beating, stagnant wages, and soulless extremes of wealth and poverty, light-bearing cracks are all that we have. They surface in unexpected places.

Take *North American Windpower* magazine, a monthly shaft of light. It was first sent to me by a friend who received it, although she never subscribed to it. When I told her how informative—and realistically hopeful—it is, she turned her non-subscription over to me.

The March 2017 issue carried the story of Lliam Hildebrand, a worker in Alberta, Canada, oil sands. Hildebrand created a national initiative, Iron and Earth, to retrain out-of-work oil sands tradespeople—among them pipefitters, electricians, boilermakers, drillers, and construction laborers—to enter the Canadian renewable technologies workforce, including solar, wind and hydro. A survey of a thousand oil sands sector workers revealed that sixty–three percent responded that they could transition directly to the renewable energy sector with some training, and fifty–nine percent reported that they were willing to take a pay cut to transition into the renewable sector. The Canadian wind company, Beothuk Energy Inc., has signed a memorandum of agreement with Iron and Earth to retrain oil and gas workers for the company's proposed offshore wind farm project, which has the potential to create forty thousand jobs.

Why not a similar US program for unemployed coal-industry workers, given that everyone knows–except then President Trump–that the cost of coal-generated electricity cannot compete with renewables and that solar and wind are the biggest job creators in electric power generation. A team of developers recently proposed to install a large solar farm atop two mountaintop removal sites in the heart of coal country, Pikeville, Kentucky. Further, they have pledged to hire as many unemployed coal miners as they can. What more prescient sign of the times than this: in April 2017, the Kentucky Coal Museum installed solar panels on its roof!

In nearby West Virginia, the Coal River Mountain Watch has been fighting to save 6,600 acres of their mountain from being blown up for strip mining of coal with a proposal for a 440-megawatt wind farm. The windpower would generate electricity for 150,000 homes, remove only 200 acres of hardwood forest, create 200 jobs with from 40 to 50 of them permanent and longer-lasting than coal jobs, and provide sustainable income for the local economy.

Remember the March 2017 photo op of President Trump surrounding himself with coal miners as he signed an executive order dismantling the Clean Power Plan with its goal of reducing carbon dioxide emissions by thirty-two percent from 2005 levels by 2030? He promised the miners that with the stroke of his pen, he would put them back to work. But the know-nothing president had not run his promise by the industry.

"You can't bring the coal industry back to where it was," retorted Robert Murray, CEO of Murray Energy Corporation, one of the largest independent operators of coal mines in the country. Moreover, Murray has "no immediate plans to reopen mines or hire miners after the order is signed," according to the May 2017 issue of *North American Windpower*.

The wind blows strong and steady in Iowa, according to Lieutenant Governor Kim Reynolds, who justifiably touts her state's goals and ambitions for renewable energy in the April, 2017 issue of *North American Windpower*. Iowa is well on the way to acquiring from forty to fifty percent of its electricity from wind turbines, the largest share of any state in the country and among the highest in the world. She notes that it is the convergence of many factors, among them, political, educational, business, and community, that fosters that state's favorable renewable-energy climate.

In 1983, Iowa passed the country's first renewable electricity standard at a time when the state was almost totally dependent on coal. Since then, Iowa's public universities, with state support, have developed strong wind-energy research programs and are educating wind-energy engineers and policymakers while community colleges are training technicians to install, service, and maintain wind turbines. As for manufacturing jobs, almost all of turbine manufacture, assembly, and installation are done by in-state companies, some of whom have re-located there. Others, such as Facebook and Google, were attracted by the abundance of renewable energy and good infrastructure. Farmers, on whose land wind turbines spin, gain a reliable revenue source in lease payments and local governments, an improved tax base for local public needs. MidAmerican Energy Company, Iowa's largest utility, envisions providing a hundred percent renewable energy for its clients.

One final thought in light of the heroic resistance of Native Americans and allies at Standing Rock Reservation, North Dakota, to a fracked oil pipeline endangering their water and sacred sites: in the northern Great Plains, one of the richest wind regimes in the world, the potential of tribal wind power exceeds three hundred gigawatts across six states, according to the US Department of Energy. That motherlode is equivalent to about half of the current electrical generating capacity in the United States.

Originally published June 4, 2017 in the *Greenfield Recorder*. Reprinted with permission.

What Then Is the Value of Bird Song?

Lost Woods: The Discovered Writings of Rachel Carson
Linda Lear, editor
Beacon Press. 1998
US Fish and Wildlife Service Blog

Lost Woods gathers some of Rachel Carson's most beautiful writings, among them "What Then Is the Value of Bird Song?"

"What Then Is the Value of Bird Song?" is steeped in mystical insight into the place where land meets sea and enriched with her depth of knowledge of the organic and inorganic marine world. But it is also fortified, as it closes, with a bracing critique of the tawdry development rapidly encroaching on the wild seacoast in the late 1950s, "the untidy litter of what passes under the name of civilization."

Carson finishes *Lost Woods* with an eloquent and urgent plea for the National Park Service to purchase and preserve shoreline areas as wilderness, not even as public parks, so there remains forever some remnant of sea, wind, and shore without human impact. Henry David Thoreau and William Blake live in her words, the former for his animus toward humans' ignorant and destructive impact on wilderness and the latter for his intuition of the immortal in the mortal, the spiritual in the material.

What strikes me in the entire collection of *Lost Woods* is the effect of her era on Carson's deepest reflection and heaviest concerns. Listening for her response to the historical period, politics, and cultural changes in the mid twentieth century United States—a response which generally rises like a coda at the end of her speeches and articles—I have noted that she is acutely preoccupied with the growing human footprint on nature and the artificial isolation of humans from nature. We learn in a letter to friends in this collection that, with the dream of preserving forested coastline as "a cathedral of stillness and peace," she was moved to help organize the Maine chapter of the Nature Conservancy.

The 1950s was an era of rapid change in the US, including:
- postwar industrial development in the United States
- rising prosperity, reduction of poverty, and growth of the middle class

- construction of the interstate highway system and consequent suburban development and sprawl
- war in Korea, and
- escalation and hardening of the Cold War

The Cold War permeated politics and civil society. It was used to support an immense buildup of conventional and nuclear arms research, testing, and development; and it engaged the two superpowers—the US and the Soviet Union—in competing militarily and economically for the allegiance of countries on every continent. The competition was responsible for internal wars and militarization within those countries, especially in Central America, Africa, and Southeast Asia. The anxiety and loss of faith reflected in letters to Carson from her readers mirrored the times. So also did her growing direct and blunt salvos about the menace to human and natural life of the arms race with the "lust for destruction" it embodied.

As a biologist and gifted naturalist who stayed close to her field of study and research, Carson was not prepared to challenge the risks posed by militarism to nature and humans with the same nuance and evidence basis of her forthcoming *Silent Spring*, 1962. Thus, her warnings in the collection sound more like a prophet's cry in the wilderness.

In 1954, Carson addressed nearly a thousand women gathered for the annual dinner of the Sorority of Women Journalists. In her talk, "The Real World Around Us," she is at ease, candid, autobiographical, and humorous—so at home, one senses, in the sisterhood of women writers. "Beauty—and all the values that derive from beauty—are not measured and evaluated in terms of the dollar," she said to her audience. She juxtaposed, more directly and comprehensively than ever, the necessity of nature for spiritual development and depth against growing trends in materialism, commercialism, suburban homogeneity, and urban artificiality.

As compelling as that verity is, though, the more recent field of ecological economics has resorted to putting a price on beauty as well as on the ecological functions of nature, to the degree they are understood, in order to argue for their preservation. Accordingly, the goods and services of nature—we might call it the global natural product—are estimated to be equivalent in worth to the global national product, some thirty-three trillion US dollars. And the economic value of a wilderness with vistas may be derived by estimating how many people would visit it and how much they are willing to pay. Nature is necessary for human survival, and preserving nature for the sake of the human economy has become the dominant paradigm for ecological preservation.

There are many difficult dilemmas posed by the necessity to impute an economic value to nature in order to preserve it.

My question for readers is:

What do we gain and what do we lose with an economic paradigm, whereby, for the sake of preserving nature? We gain

- wetlands are priced for their services in flood control and biodegradation
- marine ecosystems, for their commercial fisheries and shellfish habitats, and
- forests, for their capacity to offset CO_2 emissions from new power plants

What, then, is the value of birdsong? Does it become necessary to calculate the dollar value of the serenity and happiness that wood thrushes and veeries offer us in order to justify preserving their habitats from commercial development?

Finally, since beauty is subjective, "in the eye of the beholder," and one's sense of beauty is mediated by environment and popular culture, some may find monocultural suburban lawns beautiful and support neighborhood covenants to prohibit wildflowers and vegetables in front yards. People who grow up in cities may find forests formidable with their dark interiors and wildlife. Others, influenced by thriller movies that terrify with sharks, may experience the sea as a high-risk environment. How, then, in an increasingly urban world—in which two of three humans will live by 2050—do we sustain an intuition of beauty steeped in the natural world and the intelligence to preserve it?

Originally published the week of September 17, 2007 by the National Conservation Training Center of the US Fish and Wildlife Service at the Rachel Carson Book Club Blogspot. Reprinted with permission.

Inequality: Extreme and Growing

What does growing inequality look like?

+ a woman with no bed for the night because the local shelter is full, unable to get a job at Dunkin' Donuts because she has no address, and at the mercy of the elements and predatory men. She holds a sign with one word: *HOMELESS*
+ millions of working people holding two jobs to pay bills and, nonetheless, an illness away from bankruptcy
+ the stock market in 2020 hitting an all-time high the week of Thanksgiving while close to fourteen million children did not have enough to eat
+ the richest five hundred people on the planet adding $1.8 trillion to their wealth in 2020 amidst the COVID pandemic and surging global poverty
+ low-wage workers—mainly people of color and women— suffering most from the joint economic and medical crises of 2020
+ Native Americans, Latinos, and Blacks infected and dying disproportionately from COVID compared to whites
+ "deaths of despair" growing steadily
+ the poor and minority living in the most polluted environments of the country, increasing their vulnerability to COVID
+ the plight of women more than men in the US and across the world, for doing unpaid childcare and housework, and for being the majority of under-and low-paid service workers

- those with the deepest pockets having the principal influence on lawmakers and public policy, while the average American has almost none, and
- less happiness and community life with poorer education outcomes and health and with lower life expectancy

The Dow soars, wages don't. Inequality in a nutshell.

—Alexandria Ocasio-Cortez

Whether we focus a lens on inequality from a local, regional, or national perspective, it reflects a similar reality: the gap between rich and poor is extreme and growing. And so also are the impacts of the widening gap on health, personal debt, educational achievement, homelessness, life expectancy, and, ultimately, happiness.

I have intentionally included two similar commentaries written five years apart on the federal budget under the Democratic Obama and Republican Trump administrations, respectively. My purpose is to expose the bipartisan consensus—a consensus sustained in President Biden's 2022 proposed budget—regarding the dominance of the military in the US budget of which President Dwight D. Eisenhower warned in 1953:

Every gun that is made, every warship launched, every rocket fired signifies, in the final sense, a theft from those who hunger and are not fed, those who are cold and are not clothed.

How do we as a country reverse inequality?

- enact progressive taxation, whether on annual wealth, income, or investment gains; and close tax loopholes
- pay a living wage for all workers with no exemptions
- increase cooperative and employee-owned companies
- place employees on company boards
- rebuild the union movement
- enforce equal pay for equal and comparable work to eliminate workplace discrimination against women and people of color, and
- reduce the military budget and increase funding for real national security needs: housing, health, education, jobs, and environment

Measures toward economic justice, however, are not enough to solve social inequality. Ending violence against women, ending the extreme housing and social segregation particularly of African Americans in cities and the consequent poor public school systems in those communities, and enacting reparations to African Americans and Native Americans—are all needed to undo systemic inequality, insecurity, indignity, and injustice.

Homeless in Greenfield: A Home at the Farren?

The briefest of letters in the February 10, 2021 edition of the *Greenfield Recorder* is among the more important I have read. Elsie Gilman of Montague writes:

> Recently the *Recorder* and other newspapers are highlighting the plight of the homeless. Now that the Farren in Turners Falls will be vacant soon, why not make that into a county homeless shelter?

Instead of various groups trying to accommodate the homeless, join together staffing, funding, social services, and have enough room for all including singles, couples, and families.

Immediately I thought of Susan (not her real name). I met her on a Saturday in October 2020 when I was attending the weekly eleven-to-noon peace and democracy vigil on Greenfield Common. She was standing holding a cardboard sign with a single word—*HOMELESS*—on the concrete island of Main Street at the intersection with Federal Street. I crossed over to talk with her to see if there was any way to help. I learned she had been sleeping on the floor of a man's apartment offered to her as shelter but fled when she began to get pressure for sex in return.

When I met her, she was living in a tent with a man, a boyfriend of sorts, behind Energy Park near the railroad tracks, and the police had recently picked him up for prior charges. I was gripped by fear for her vulnerability, living as she was in a tent alone in a dark, out-of-the way place with one other homeless person in a nearby tent. She felt comfortable with him because he was gay.

Each subsequent Saturday late morning we talked—about where she could get free meals, housing before the winter, and security from the streets, although very little about her past. She kept that vague.

She knew the schedule for church meals in Greenfield, breakfast at ServiceNet Shelter, and a shower at another place I did not recognize. She had applied to ServiceNet Shelter for housing, but there were twenty-five others ahead of her on the waiting list. She applied for jobs at Dunkin' Donuts and Dollar Store, but her lack of address gave them pause to hire her. Her healthcare was nonexistent, and I still don't know how she got pain medication for her severe toothache.

We also talked about what hopes she had for herself: a GED and then a certificate from GCC in some area of healthcare. From my prior experience of coaching someone for the GED math component, I know it is not a piece of cake and would be a setup for failure without intensive tutoring.

As the season moved into November I worried about where she would sleep when winter took hold. Late November, not seeing her at the intersection, I went looking for her tent by the railroad tracks: all I could think about was another woman and man who died in January 2019 in a tent in Greenfield from carbon monoxide poisoning. Susan's tent was gone. As it turned out, the only help I could give her was some money each Saturday when we met—sometimes for food, often for warmer clothes and for a second sleeping bag to double up in the cold of her tent.

I will never forget when she nodded toward my companions with their peace and democracy and Black Lives Matter signs on the common at the eleven-to-noon vigil and said, "I like what you're doing."

I sent an email to the mayor and her assistant and to church-affiliated people about Susan, a young woman who stood at that intersection signifying many homeless throughout Franklin County. No one responded.

Elsie Gilman's letter could not have been timelier. The Farren Care Center in Montague will soon be vacant. It may still be somewhat habitable whereas other large vacant buildings left to languish are discouragingly expensive to rehab. Having been a residential physical and mental health care center, the Farren may be more suitable for redesign as housing for those now homeless.

A critically needed exploration of homelessness and call to action, Housing Is a Human Right, was launched. Planned by Greening Greenfield and Franklin County Continuing the Political Revolution, the housing forum will examine the problem of homelessness and lack of affordable housing in Franklin County and discuss options and opportunities for housing the homeless and creating affordable housing in Franklin County in eight virtual workshops.

Why not dedicate a workshop to explore the potential reuse of the Farren for housing the homeless, with participants including the owner, person in charge of building maintenance, and a town representative? A good beginning was the workshop on Abandoned Buildings in the Housing Is a Human Right conference with local government representatives from Montague, Greenfield, and Athol participating.

Following the completion of their eight workshops, the organizers of Housing Is a Human Right formed working groups in June 2021 on various housing topics, among them homelessness and conversion of vacant buildings into affordable and/ or housing for the homeless. The Town of Montague has been in conversation about reuse of the building with the owner of the Farren Care Center, Trinity Health, with no firm decisions as of late June 2021.

Originally published February 17, 2021 in the *Greenfield Recorder*. Reprinted with permission.

Inequality and Its Consequences

In her *Recorder* news article "Local Gun Business Booming," Anita Fritz related that gun sales hit record highs in western Massachusetts in late 2020.

Norman Emond Jr., owner of The Gun Rack in Turners Falls, reported, "selling an unprecedented number of guns" and "struggling to keep up with demand." He estimated that eighty percent were for protection and twenty percent, recreation. Given the state of the country, he explained, "people are unsure, scared, and want to be ready for whatever."

Ed Hallett, co-owner of Bear Arms in Orange, concurred as the shop experienced record new customers and new sales, beginning in March 2020. Correspondingly, Overwatch Outpost in Charlemont had eighty-five percent more sales than the year before the pandemic.

All shop owners attested that gun sales go up before a federal election, but the 2020 election year was unique. The rise in gun purchase in western Massachusetts paralleled the same surge across the country. The research company Small Arms Analytics tracks gun sales and reported that the estimated number of handguns and long guns sold in the United States through the end of September 2020—nearly seventeen million—is "not only more than 2019, it's more than any full year in the years since 2000 we have records for."

It's an axiom that the gun industry flourishes in a culture of fear and insecurity. We can only conclude that the out-of-control pandemic, the threat of robbery given record unemployment, and fear of violence during the election combined with an increasingly bitter political divide since the Trump presidency fed national fear and insecurity.

Given that the United States is the wealthiest country in the world, able to afford all the resources to secure its citizens economically, socially, and medically, why so much insecurity and fear?

I found some answers to the question in *The Inner Level: How More Equal Societies Reduce Stress, Restore Sanity, and Improve Everyone's Well-Being* by respected research authors Richard Wilkinson and Kate Pickett. They have compared the United States with similar democracies, including those of Western Europe and Asia, and concluded that while we are the wealthiest of the democracies, we are the most economically and socially unequal.

Economic equality measures the gap in income and wealth between the rich and the not rich. How far apart is the top one percent in wealth from the bottom fifty percent of our country, for example, or the top ten percent from the bottom ten percent? *In fact, the top one percent of US households has more wealth than the bottom fifty percent combined.*

As an extreme example of US economic inequality, in 2020 the stock market hit an all-time high for that year the week of Thanksgiving while just four months earlier close to fourteen million children did not have enough to eat. Concurrently, as the investor class was raking in thousands to millions of dollars in profit, nearly eight hundred thousand people filed for unemployment benefits for the first time in late fall 2020, as unemployment payments ran out for many millions.

Compared with other well-to-do, developed countries, the United States ranks highest in income inequality and correspondingly ranks highest in ill health and social problems. Studies find that large gaps in society between the rich and the not-rich contribute to stress, loss of community life, mental disorders, poorer physical health, abuse of alcohol and drugs, and greater violence.

Across all racial groups, the average number of years US people live has been dropping since 2014, due in large part to the increase in suicides and drug and alcohol overdoses among midlife adults. By September 2019, income inequality in the United States had reached its highest level in fifty years.

Given there is no magic bullet, no weapon, no gun shop that can solve our state of social fear and insecurity, how, then, can we grow economic democracy to reduce income inequality and personal insecurity? Here's a beginning list of recommendations:

- enact progressive taxation, that is, higher taxes on wealth and more generous benefits for employees
- pay a living wage
- increase cooperative and employee-owned companies
- place employees on company boards of directors
- rebuild the union movement, and
- enforce equal pay for equal and comparable work to eliminate workplace discrimination against women and people of color

Such proposed initiatives for more equal—both economically and socially—workplaces have been studied and shown to increase worker productivity, satisfaction, and innovation.

I welcome you to add your own.

Originally published December 3, 2020 in the *Greenfield Recorder*. Reprinted with permission.

Bring Our War Dollars Home

What do our income taxes pay for?

Our federal income taxes pay for *mandatory* federal budget programs, including Social Security and Medicare, and for interest on national debt. They also pay for *discretionary* budget programs, among them education, housing, energy, environment, transportation, food and agriculture, and defense.

"The budget is a profoundly moral document," stated Paul Begala, a former adviser to President Clinton. "for where your treasure is, there will your heart be."

Let's look, then, at where the Obama Administration proposed to spend its treasure—our taxes—fiscal year 2016, from October 1, 2016 to September 30, 2017:

+ at a time when there were no challenges to US military supremacy, seventy percent of our country's fiscal 2016 proposed trillion-dollar discretionary budget would go to national defense—Pentagon, Homeland Security, intelligence, nuclear weapons, and other armaments, ordnance, and military weapons
+ five percent would go to housing and community development, six percent to education, and two percent to transportation, whose infrastructure had been consistently graded D+ by the American Society of Civil Engineers and only continues to decay
+ the proposed budget for the state department, responsible for diplomacy and resolution of international conflict—such as the *win-without-war* negotiations with Iran over their curbing their nuclear weapons capacity—is less than seven percent of the entire defense budget, and
+ the Pentagon has more than seventy times the budget of the US Environmental Protection Agency charged with environmental health and regulating greenhouse gases to slow climate change, a genuine threat to our country and the world

Why are nearly fifty million Americans—mostly women and children—living in poverty while we spent a million dollars in fiscal 2015 per soldier per year in the failed and futile war in Afghanistan?

That, our longest war, has resolved nothing: 2014 was the bloodiest year in terms of Afghani deaths since we initiated it in 2001.

The trillions of dollars poured into the reckless Iraq and Afghanistan wars might as well have been shredded, observed one defense analyst. And yet, in its twenty-first-century long-term plans, the Pentagon prepares for fighting battles anywhere and everywhere it deems necessary on all continents except Antarctica despite growing consensus that our war on terrorism has destabilized countries and resulted in greater numbers of terrorists.

While we lead the world in global military spending and global weapons sales, in 2015 the US ranked thirty-fourth of thirty-five developed countries ranked on the well-being of children, according to the UN. Compared to all countries, we ranked thirty-fifth in life expectancy, thirty-fourth in infant mortality, seventeenth in education, and thirty-seventh in health care.

Of all Western countries, the United States is the most unequal in wealth. We police the world from more than 800 military bases and with US Special Forces operating in 134 countries while we sacrifice our quality of education, a living wage, equity in pay for women and people of color, infrastructure, and efforts to reverse climate change.

Why are our cities—Central Falls, Rhode Island; Stockton California; and Detroit—going bankrupt with more coming while we give military aid and assistance to countries that don't need it—Israel, countries that abuse human rights—Bahrain, and countries whose armies use child soldiers—Democratic Republic of Congo, Somalia, Yemen, Chad, South Sudan?

Some ninety years ago, Brigadier General Smedley D. Butler published a small book, *War Is a Racket*. To paraphrase Butler's blunt critique, war is first and foremost about making the world safe for war profits. It is the oldest, most profitable racket, in which billions of dollars are earned for millions of lives destroyed. More than twenty-one thousand new American millionaires and billionaires emerged from the human ashes of World War I, while the federal government was mired in post-war debt—a debt paid for by the treasure of working people's taxes.

In a 1949 speech, General Omar Bradley succinctly observed about the American atomic bombing of Japan: "Ours is a world of nuclear giants and ethical infants. We know more about war than we know about peace, more about killing than about living."

Almost sixty years ago, President Eisenhower presciently warned:

> The cost of one modern bomber is this: a modest brick school in more than sixty cities; two electric power plants, each serving a town of sixty-thousand; two fine, fully equipped hospitals. This is not a way of life at all in any true sense. It is humanity hanging from a cross of iron.

At the height of the Vietnam War, Martin Luther King deepened Eisenhower's warning:

> A nation that spends more money on military defenses than on programs of social uplift is approaching spiritual death.

We must—as the US mayors' conference and the majority of US citizens from all political persuasions have called for—reorder our priorities and bring the war dollars home into our communities for health, education, living wage jobs, rebuilding infrastructure, and environmental protection. Simply put: *downsize the global military mission and rebuild a healthy civilian economy.*

As for jobs lost in downsizing the military, a study by the Political Economy Research Institute at University of Massachusetts, Amherst, finds that one billion dollars spent on clean energy, healthcare, and education compared to the same money spent on defense creates a larger number of jobs with mid- to high-range salaries and benefits. Bath Iron Works, Maine's largest employer, has retooled some of its manufacturing of naval destroyers into developing deep-water, offshore wind power. The state of Maine's goal is to lead the country in wind power and production systems.

Genuine existential threats to our national security do exist. Among them are the extreme financial gap between rich and poor, the gap in education between rich and poor, the hemorrhaging of jobs that pay a living wage and benefits, the specter of climate change—all of which are felt most deeply by the shrinking middle class, working class, and poor. We urgently need a national discussion in thousands of local forums with our politicians—

Democrat and Republican—who have systemically stymied all serious attempts to significantly reduce the nation's defense budget.

Budgets are profound moral documents. Our national treasure is being spent on entitlement programs for corporate defense contractors and the Pentagon while we fail our citizens in "social uplift."

Our government is in heart failure.

Originally published April 4, 2015 in the *Greenfield Recorder*. Reprinted with permission.

Winners: Wars, Walls, and Wealthy
Losers: Diplomacy, Public Health, and Environment

Budgets are moral documents—or immoral, depending on priorities. So also is tax policy.

Consider the $1.3 trillion discretionary budget Trump proposed for 2021. In snapshot, the Pentagon got fifty-five percent and every other need of 331 million people—from health, education, agriculture, transportation, environmental protection to housing— was left with forty-five percent. As one retired colonel observed, "The military gravy train is running at full speed." The bipartisan approved budget for 2021 had a similar proportion of spending favoring militarism over human needs as Trump's proposed budget.

Military weapons makers are the biggest winners, raking in nearly one-half of every Pentagon dollar, an estimated $350 billion, annually. Moreover, in the midst of the coronavirus epidemic, the Pentagon increased periodic progress payments made to military manufacturers to keep them on schedule, a move described as a "taxpayer rip-off" by one retired Pentagon official.

Military corporations, though, trump military personnel. Tens of thousands of soldiers and their families rely on food stamps. For at least two weeks after our country was advised to implement social distancing, army and marine soldiers, against their own fears, were compelled to continue training in close mass formation. Paralyzed by indecision, mid-level leaders were waiting for higher command decisions. US Army aviation aircrews were ordered not to wear masks, use disinfectant, or follow medical guidelines when airlifting coronavirus patients to local hospitals. With no official plans to quarantine the crew, crew members talked of taking off doors while in flight.

Two other winners are Immigration and Customs Control, ICE, and its sister agency, Customs and Border Patrol, CBP.

Under Trump's proposed budget, ICE–the agency whose agents seize parents from their jobs and homes for deportation–would double by 2024. Trump's proposed 2021 CBP budget would have gone from $14.8 billion to $15.6 billion to bolster snatching babies and children from their parents at the US-Mexican border and caging them in crowded, unsanitary conditions. Budget priorities also included $2.3 billion investments in militarized border security technology, infrastructure, and equipment, new border fencing, and hiring an additional 750 Border Patrol agents.

Another Winner: Wealth

The 2017 tax cut–hyped as a bonus for all–has left our government with a multi-billion dollar debt that could have funded the missing coronavirus test kits, medical safety equipment, vaccine research, and urgently needed basic health care.

Thanks to the tax cut–the rich get richer: seventy-two percent of the tax cuts were directed to the wealthiest twenty percent of households. Ninety-one of the flourishing Fortune 500 companies paid no income taxes in 2018, and most of the rest paid half the rate they ought to have paid by tax regulation.

Trump's proposed budget prized corporate life over human life, militarized security and walls over tackling the challenge of a humanistic immigration policy, and the wealthy over the rest of us. Another gift to corporate America involved granting Gilead Sciences the exclusive right to research the drug Remdesivir that shows potential for treating the coronavirus. If successful, the company was guaranteed a seven-year patent, could set price controls on it and benefit from grants and tax credits, and could block manufacturers from developing generic versions at lower costs more affordable for patients.

Losers in Trump's Budget

US State Department: If Trump had his way, the state department might have been cut by twenty-three percent in 2021, thus undermining potentially more effective and intelligent response to conflict, such as diplomacy and humanitarian aid. Why not build our diplomacy capacity, given we have failed wretchedly in war since World War II in Korea, Vietnam, Afghanistan, the second Iraq War, and Syria, leaving millions dead, injured physically and spiritually, homeless, and hungry. Even a majority of US veterans doubt that the trillion–dollar wars they fought in Afghanistan, Iraq, and Syria were worth fighting.

The Environmental Protection Agency: Trump's proposed cut of twenty-seven percent was nothing less than insane, given increased coastline flooding and erosion, more extreme wildfires, worsened hurricanes, and prolonged droughts from the climate crisis, all climate-related disasters estimated to cripple economic growth in the 2020s and beyond. Further, researchers calculated that eighty thousand additional lives would be lost every decade if the Trump administration completed its rollback of clean air protections—all to coddle some well-connected fossil fuel, auto, and truck corporations.

Health and Human Services: Trump's proposed cut of nine percent to the US Department of Health and Human Services, including a sixteen percent cut to the Centers for Disease Control, would have been homicidal. Local and state health departments across the country have lost nearly a quarter of their workforce–frontline health workers critical to stemming the spread of the virus–since 2008, when their positions were eliminated during the Great Recession.

Epidemiologist Larry Brilliant, who helped eradicate smallpox, underscored our underfunded and underprepared public health system: "By the time South Korea had done two hundred thousand COVID-19 tests, we had probably done less than one thousand."

Among twenty peer countries, all well-to-do, developed, and industrialized, the United States has the largest number of opioid users per capita, the highest drug-death rate, the highest use of anti-depressants per capita, and the highest suicide and homicide rates. In additional comparisons of health with comparable countries, we have the highest infant mortality rate and the shortest life expectancy.

Why do we fail in protecting our own people's health and well-being while we squander nearly a trillion dollars each year–with the assent of both Republicans and Democrats–on maintaining a failed and futile military empire across the world?

Now what could be done to chart a better future for the ninety-nine percent?

- repeal the 2017 tax cuts
- invest in diplomacy, lower the defense budget
- retrain workers for the Green New Deal as described in the publication *Warheads to Windmills, How to Pay for the Green New Deal* by Timmon Wallis
- *quarantine* fossil fuels where they are–in the ground
- restore the capacity of our health and environmental agencies to at least pre-2008 recession levels
- enact universal health coverage, and
- heed the March 2020 call of UN Secretary General Guterres:

> *Put armed conflict on lockdown and focus together on the true fight of our lives—the pandemic.*

Originally published May 30, 2020 at *Portside*. Reprinted with permission.

More Equal Societies
The Inner Level: How More Equal Societies Reduce Stress, Restore Sanity, and Improve Everyone's Well-Being
by Richard Wilkinson and Kate Picket
Penguin Press. 2019

> *The five hundred richest people in the world . . . gained a combined $1.2 trillion in wealth in 2019, further exacerbating inequities that have not been seen since the late 1920s. Eight of the ten richest people in the world are from the US.*
>
> —*The Inner Level*

If all that you do is view one simple line graph on page three of *The Inner Level*, you will grasp the authors' stark and consistent findings, namely, that income inequality in developed countries is directly linked with–drives, in fact–much of the health and social ills of those societies. In essence this graph conveys that as income inequality—or the gap in income between the richest and the poorest of a country—increases, the health and social well-being of its citizens decline.

As *The Inner Level* both documents and generously discusses, rising income inequality leads to a plague of ills: higher rates of people in prison, higher teenage birth rates, higher rates of mental illness, more child neglect and children bullying other children, higher rates of homicide, lower educational performance, and lower life expectancy, that is, the average number of years that people live.

The United States ranks highest in income inequality, manifest in the graph, and correspondingly ranks highest in ill health and social problems compared with other rich, developed countries. And, conversely, the Scandinavian countries and Japan, which score lowest on income inequality, fare best in health and social well-being. Moreover, the same pattern prevails among all of the fifty US states.

The average number of years US people live has been dropping since 2014, due in large part to the increase in suicides and drug and alcohol overdoses among midlife adults, across all racial groups.

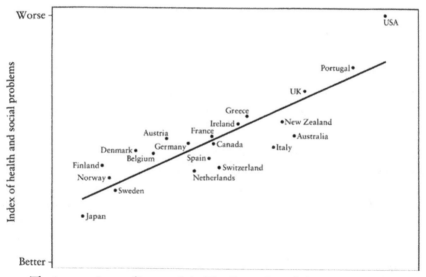

The income inequality graph in The Inner Level *demonstrates that income inequality in developed countries drives much of the health and social ills of those societies.*

photo courtesy of *The Inner Level*

Parallel with that tragic trend is increasing income inequality: by September 2019, income inequality in the United States had reached its highest level in fifty years. Taking a larger perspective, Wilkinson and Pickett link all recent global financial crises, political polarizations, nativism, growing refugee and migration trends, and rapidly worsening climate crisis in part to the global trend in inequality: "Inequality has made no small contribution to all of these."

The arc of concern across *The Inner Level* is the social environment and how it is impacted by economic inequality—specifically how economic dominance and subordination contribute to stress, loss of community life, mental disorders, poorer physical health, abuse of alcohol and drugs, and greater violence. But the authors emphatically state, "This is not a self-help book. We need to understand the receptors of social pain before we can recognize the structural causes of that pain."

Why have young students and adults across the United States reported dramatic increases in anxiety in surveys from the 1950s through the 1990s? Mental disorders associated with anxiety parallel that trend as do the number of people disabled by mental disorders who qualify for Social Security Disability Insurance.

The authors link those trends in anxiety and resulting mental disability to the finding that "community life is weaker in societies with bigger income differences between the rich and the poor." Greater income differences make class differences more stark and more powerfully felt by those less equal. Social status is more stratified in more unequal societies, and the distance in social echelons among classes is increased. Material wealth, conspicuously on display in more unequal societies, increasingly replaces inner well-being as the measure of one's worth.

Not surprisingly, community life, measured by involvement in local groups, voluntary organizations, and civic associations—often called social cohesion—is more prevalent in more equal societies. That, in turn, feeds social trust and helps explain why rates of homicide are consistently lower in more equal societies.

To their credit, the authors transition from how income inequality ravages the human spirit and the well-being of a society to how it concomitantly weakens human motivation and activism on behalf of environmental sustainability. While income inequality fosters status anxiety, consumerism, individualism, and social dysfunction, the climate crisis requires our "acting on the basis of the common good as never before, indeed acting for the good of humanity as a whole." Wilkinson and Pickett conclude with an ominous warning: unless we reduce economic inequality, "we may have to accept that we will be defeated by climate change."

The authors, prolific researchers and writers for many years on the theme of *The Inner Level*, point out that their conclusions on the effects of growing economic inequality are amplified by findings of hundreds of other researchers. Since the 1970s, when the first studies on the subject were published, hundreds of subsequent studies have consistently found that the larger the income gap between rich and poor, the higher the social dysfunction. Moreover, inequality in income drives poorer human and social well-being *for all* in society including those at the top, but it is always the poorest who bear the worst burdens.

While *The Inner Level* is impressively comprehensive in its scope and latitude, it is, at the same time, single-dimensioned, while societies the authors study are not. There is next to nothing regarding the statistics and effects of economic inequality between men and women and between races, and not because those more-dimensioned realities of inequality have not been studied and quantified. Put starkly in a recent Oxfam report, "the richest twenty-two men in the world own more wealth than all the women in Africa."

A team of researchers, including security-studies experts and statisticians, has created the largest global database on the status of women. Called WomanStats, the database enables researchers to compare the security and level of conflict within 175 countries to the overall security of women in those countries. The findings are profoundly illuminating for global security and world peace. The degree of equality of women, including economic equality, within countries predicts best—better than degree of democracy and better than level of wealth, income inequality or ethno-religious identity—how peaceful or conflict-ridden their countries are. Further, democracies with higher levels of violence against women are less stable and more likely to choose force rather than diplomacy to resolve conflict.

Inheritance and property laws that deprive women of resources comparable to those inherited by their brothers and husbands ultimately impoverish women through a form of economic violence. Because women's reproduction and care for children and extended family–estimated at $10.8 trillion worldwide–are not compensated, women are cheated of savings, pensions, and, in the United States, Social Security. Consequently, the greatest risk factor for being poor in old age is having been a mother.

Rampant discriminatory workplace policies that deny women equal pay for equal work and merited promotions are societal forms of economic violence against women. Worse for working mothers in many countries is the persistent motherhood penalty whereby they are further set back financially by lack of paid parental leave and government-funded child care.

If the authors had considered the stark fact that nearly two-thirds of the minimum wage workers in the United States are women, a wage that consigns them to poverty, they would have featured the "Fight for $15" campaign and its advocacy of a fifteen-dollar US minimum wage among their structural recommendations to reduce income inequality.

Economic violence against women results in income inequality compounded throughout their lives and in old age. And that inequality is worsened by racial inequality. Progress in closing the earnings gap between men and women has also slowed considerably, according to the Institute for Women's Policy Research, which states:

> If the pace of change in the annual earnings ratio were to continue at the same rate as it has since 1984, it would take until 2059 for women and men to reach earnings parity, *and substantially longer for women of color.* Black women's median annual earnings would reach parity with White men's in 2119, and Hispanic women's in 2224.

If progress has slowed so considerably, might it not even stop altogether?

The Inner Level would have been enriched and made more meaningful by including the documented greater inequality suffered by women and people of color and the slowing pace to re-right it. Likewise, the authors' structural recommendations for economic justice would have been more substantively grounded in the workplace misogyny and racism faced by women and people of color in their struggle for equality.

Originally published December 20, 2020 at *Portside*. Reprinted with permission.

International Relations and the Golden Rule

On its last page, *Farmers' Almanac 2020* carried versions of the Golden Rule from all major religions and spiritual traditions. Here is a sample.

Buddhism

Hurt not others in ways you yourself would find hurtful.

Judaism

What is hateful to you, do not do to your fellow man.
That is the entire law; the rest is commentary.

Islam

No one of you is a believer until he desires for his brother
that which he desires for himself.

Confucianism

Surely it is the maxim of loving-kindness:
Do not unto others what you would not have them do unto you.

Christianity

All things whatsoever ye would that men should do to you,
do ye even to them, for this is the law of the prophets.

It may seem a stretch, naïve even, to apply the Golden Rule to our own government's policies toward other peoples and governments, but that is precisely what the United Nations intended in the Universal Declaration of Human Rights proclaimed on December 10, 1948. Appointed by President Harry S Truman, Eleanor Roosevelt chaired the UN Commission on Human Rights and presided over the drafting of that declaration, deemed one of the most important documents in history.

One brief sentence from a much longer preamble to the humanistic declaration embodies its essence: *"It is essential to promote the development of friendly relations between nations."*

Perhaps no other initiative by an American president strove so high to promote peaceful relations with an enemy—the Soviet Union at the height of the Cold War—than John F. Kennedy's speech on nuclear disarmament at American University in May 1963:

> I am talking about genuine peace, the kind of peace that makes life on earth worth living, the kind that enables men and nations to grow and to hope and build a better life for their children—not merely peace for Americans but peace for all men and women— not merely peace in our time but peace for all time.

The following articles revolve around the spirit of the Golden Rule. Some concern violation of the Golden Rule in US foreign policy and actions toward certain countries and peoples, namely Cuba and Vietnam and Venezuela, Muslims, and Central American refugees. Others document the Traprock Center for Peace and Justice's initiatives to live the Golden Rule through proactive partnerships created with community-based organizations in Vietnam and Sierra Leone.

The administration of President Joe Biden began quickly to undo animosity and hatred that infected the Trump administration toward Muslims and Central American refugees at the US border with Mexico. The new president quickly signed executive orders to reunite children separated from parents, to revamp the asylum system for the thousands of asylum seekers forced to remain in Mexico, to craft a path to citizenship for immigrants, and to end the Muslim Ban. Trump supporters, particularly within the US Department of Homeland Security, immediately challenged those humane initiatives issued in the first two weeks of Biden's administration. Tom Homan, Trump's 2017-2018 Immigration and Customs Enforcement director and hard-liner on immigration, was quoted in the February 3, 2021 *New York Times*: morale within the agency had been "flushed down the toilet," given that many ICE agents favored Trump's perspective on immigrants at our southern border. He forecasted that Biden's immigration policies would be undermined from within.

Thus far, there is no change in the brutal economic punishment that the US government has heaped on the socialist countries of Cuba and Venezuela.

Memories of Muslim and Arab Friends

Donald Trump's odious, ugly American pledge in 2016 to prohibit Muslims from entering our country stirred long-cherished memories of my Muslim and Arab students and friends.

I am looking at two small cream-colored pillows nestled into corners of our living room chairs. They are embossed with arabesque designs on their borders and silver filigree threading at the pillow's edges. For more than twenty-five years, the pillows have poignantly recalled a Muslim student, Ali, whom I taught at MIT. He was older than other students, the chief of police in Karachi, Pakistan on a yearlong fellowship.

My lasting memories of Ali are his quiet, solid respect when we spoke—in startling contrast to my expectations of a chief of police. But I was his professor, and as I found with future Muslim students, they generally hold their teachers with a regard rarely found in US students. Our conversations after morning class finished quickly when it was time for prayer: he prayed multiple times daily on a prayer rug with other Muslims at MIT in a room designated for them.

With regard and something akin to humility, he bowed and presented me the gift of those pillows at semester's end.

Yared was a public health officer for his town in rural Ethiopia who came to the Boston University School of Public Health in the late 1990s for a master's degree in environmental health. I specialized there in urban environmental health and environmental justice in low-income communities of color, working on issues of healthy public housing, asthma, lead poisoning, and community gardening.

Yared spoke little in class yet listened with pensive intensity, extrapolating–I would discern in time–all that he learned about urban poverty, food deserts in inner cities, poor housing conditions to water safety, pesticide use, and sanitation issues that he faced in his work at home.

I will always remember the image of that quietly dignified man when he entered my office at the end of the semester to thank me for what he had learned: he put his hands together in a prayer-like posture and bowed slightly, a timeless gesture and gift of respect. In our last conversation, he recounted charmingly that he had learned that American couples spend a weekend alone from time to time, leaving their children with friends or family. And thus, he planned to meet his wife in the capital city Addis Ababa on his first weekend home while relatives cared for their children.

Rana, a student from Lebanon, energized our department of environmental health with her passion for learning. With iron-willed insistence, she overcame every obstacle put in her way in order to gain entry into the department's doctoral program, including taking many science and statistics pre-requisites. Throughout her five years at Boston University, I watched her weave her unique interests in society and environment as she merged social and economic dimensions of community health with environmental health science into an original dissertation.

Rana observed Ramadan with discipline and nary a complaint of hunger in contrast to 1960s Catholic students, myself included, who sought exemptions from fasting during Lent. I will always treasure the conversation Rana and I had in the quiet of my office when she told me that there was a Sufi—one who lives the inner mystical dimension of Islam—within me.

Siti, an Indonesian lawyer, greeted my partner and me at Adisucipto International Airport in Yogyakarta, Indonesia, where we arrived for a working session on the health effects of prostitution, a project of the international NGO Coalition Against Trafficking in Women, which my partner directed. Siti's small stature belied her sizable achievements, among them founding a women's crisis center for battered women and creating a course on gender and Islam at the Institute of Islamic Studies where she taught.

A Muslim feminist to her core, she insisted on an agreement before marrying her husband that she make her own decisions and have her own career. Together, they were raising a daughter who at seven years old was spirited, curious, bright, and brimming with promise. She adopted us immediately as her aunties, an Asian tradition of welcome and warmth for friends whom they take in as family.

I met Christine, a Syrian Catholic nun, in the early 1970s when we were graduate students at an institute of Louvain University in Brussels, Belgium. The image of her raising her head and exclaiming lyrically "la belle Syrie"—the beautiful Syria—as she relayed stories of her life in Damascus has never left me. Often in late morning while we were studying in our adjacent rooms, she would brew dark, thick coffee in a copper pot and invite me to share it with her. A small china cup embossed with gold leaf and desert flowers–her gift to me–holds those absorbing morning conversations rich in images of the country she loved.

"Je suis Arabe," I am Arab, she would say proudly every now and then, and I imagined a landscape of light and desert and ancient Arab architecture in her smiling bronze face.

Those Muslim and Arab friends enriched and expanded my sense of being a citizen of the world, as one of the founders of the United States Thomas Paine, wrote of himself. His exact words: *The world is my country, all mankind are my brethren, and to do good is my religion.* His is wisdom for our insular country, deporting, as I write, women and children fleeing from violence in their Central American countries.

Originally published March 2, 2016 in the *Daily Hampshire Gazette*. Reprinted with permission.

Cuba Reflections

What is Cuba like?

Since visiting there in 2017, I have been asked the question hundreds of times and learned that every third person harbors a desire to visit there.

Yes, there are iconic '57 Chevrolets, some in mint condition, for taking tourists around Havana. But most 1950s Russian and

American cars there would not pass emissions and safety inspections here. There are no traffic jams in that city of 2.2 million people because most Cubans take buses, ride bikes, use pedicabs, and walk. Music—especially Afro Cuban and salsa—is everywhere: in hotels, small clubs, plazas, flowing from opened windows. So no need to go in search of it. It finds you.

Cubans love books, we were told. Sure enough, there are many bookstores in Havana. Could their love of books stem from a public education system free of charge through university and medical school, the most democratic educational system in the Americas? Within two years after the 1959 revolution, Cuba's aggressive literacy program, which placed special focus on women, Afro-Cubans, and rural people, reached ninety-six percent of adults and schoolchildren. It stands at one hundred percent in 2021. By contrast, thirty-two million adults in the US are considered illiterate, reflecting the fact that our country invests much less of our GDP in education than does Cuba.

Every morning just after seven, the streets filled with children in school uniforms walking, being biked, and, in the case of small rural towns like Boca de Camarioca where we stayed, being brought in horse-drawn carriages to their schools.

In Havana, we met with two key women's organizations, the Federation of Cuban Women and the National Union of Cuban Women Lawyers. They described their primary- and secondary-school programs on violence against women and have a profound understanding of prostitution and the sexual exploitation of women. We learned that their feminist magazines—one for girls and one for women—reach hundreds of thousands of readers.

Cuba is a poor country, with the average monthly salary of teachers forty dollars at the time of our visit and no evident signs of consumerism—no shopping malls, luxury goods, cheap fast-food places, or billboard advertising. Despite its poverty, it has the lowest malnutrition rate in the Americas.

Nowhere did I see homeless people sleeping in parks, doorways, or under bridges nor people begging as I saw daily during the years I worked in Boston. Boston, with a quarter of Havana's population, had nearly eight thousand homeless men, women, and children in 2016, with a twenty-five percent increase in homeless families between 2015 and 2016.

The US embargo of Cuba, more accurately called a *bloqueo* or blockade by Cubans, began in 1960 with the intent to deny money and supplies to the country, decrease wages, and to "bring about hunger, desperation and the overthrow of the [Castro] government," according to a state department memo. And, yes, there is a sense of the country locked in the 1950s with housing and colonial buildings desperately in need of repair, extremely crowded buses, shortages of consumer goods, and poor air quality in Havana. Years of material deprivation, amazingly, have not dampened the warmth, affection, and welcome that everyone who visits Cuba speaks of, richness in the Cuban spirit sustained, possibly, by the more equal society.

Since 2011, the Cuban government under Rául Castro allowed small private enterprises to open. Families rent rooms and offer meals to tourists in what are called *casas particulares*. Those and other small microenterprises were flourishing and raising incomes and standards of living across the island.

One hallmark of Cuba's achievements is its free healthcare system, recognized as one of the best in the world, as well as the primary care it provides in poor communities throughout the world. In meeting with healthcare providers, we learned of their emphasis on disease prevention and the country's policy that every community, no matter how remote, has a primary care facility. With its commitment to healthcare as a human right, Cuba has achieved higher life expectancy and a lower infant mortality rate than the United States, key indicators of the overall health of the country's people.

As in many colonial-era countries, Cuba's wealth was built on the African slave trade and slave labor. One factor that may contribute to Cubans' overall health achievements is that social and economic integration of black and white Cubans—an intentional goal since their revolution—is more advanced than that of many countries, including (and especially) our own. In 2015, two years before our visit, black and Hispanic households in the United States had, on average, one-tenth the money and property of white households.

President Obama made a trip to Cuba in 2015 after much closed-door negotiation facilitated at times by the Vatican and consultation with wealthy Miami Cuban-American businessmen. Some of them joined him in Havana, flown there on the private jet of a Cuban-American healthcare billionaire.

Obama's intentions did appear honorable–opening up Cuba's economy with private enterprise to raise the standard of living, releasing political prisoners, and encouraging free elections. Yet there is a fatal irony in those objectives for Cuba. US so-called free national elections are determined by money–the biggest spenders win. We have the largest prison system in the world with a disproportionate number of African Americans unjustly incarcerated, and we have never yet, as a society, come to terms with structural racism, our segregated cities, and segregated urban schools. Even with the Affordable Care Act, medical expenses are the biggest cause of bankruptcies while executives in the healthcare industry become multimillionaires.

Realistically, most US people would not choose to live in Cuba: we have more individual freedoms and no shortages of consumer items, if you can afford them. I do remember, however, a sign scrawled on a wall in the city of Matanzas, former center of the African slave trade, that speaks to the island country's social aspirations: *la dignidad no se vende*, Dignity is not for sale.

Originally published March 14, 2017 in the *Greenfield Recorder*. Reprinted with permission.

Economic Sanctions: War by Another Name

In early 2019, the White House threatened to invade Venezuela, take down the government, and replace it with the Trump administration's choice of president and political party. Though no missiles were fired and no bombs dropped on the country, our government was waging a war by other means, namely criminal economic sanctions, to achieve the same end. And sanctions are just as lethal as missiles and bombs.

Economic sanctions kill people by weakening the economy in public and private sectors, causing job and income loss, and reducing people's access to food, medicine, medical supplies, and healthcare.

Sanctions against Venezuela began with President Obama in 2015. However, the most crippling and deadly were ordered since by Trump. They have not been lifted by President Biden.

In August 2017, Trump prohibited Venezuela from borrowing in US financial markets, thus preventing its economy from recovering from a deep recession caused in part by the global drop in oil prices. The US financial embargo produced rapid decline in Venezuela's oil production, extreme drop in export income, and loss of access to credit. Consequently, revenue for critically needed imports for health, agriculture, and industry plummeted. Two respected US economists, Mark Weisbrot and Jeffrey Sachs, estimated that those sanctions caused forty thousand deaths in 2017-2018.

In January 2019. Trump tightened the noose with sanctions intended to prevent Venezuela's government-owned oil industry from exporting oil to the US and the rest of the world, the goal to strangle the economy, given ninety percent of Venezuela's exports was crude oil. Those sanctions also froze billions of dollars of overseas Venezuelan assets, including gold reserves that the government might have sold to stabilize the economy.

In August 2019, Trump expanded existing sanctions, prohibiting any American economic transactions with Venezuela and threatening economic sanctions against any foreign company doing business with Venezuela.

One ex-CIA official captured the imperialist logic of those sanctions: "Put pressure on the target government by ripping out the social and economic fabric of the country. Make people suffer as much as you can until the country plunges into chaos, until at some point you can step in and impose your choice of government on that country."

The leading Venezuelan economist, Francisco Rodriguez (an opponent of the current President Nicolás Maduro), estimated that Venezuela had suffered the largest economic collapse of a country "not at war" nor experiencing oil strikes, since the 1970s. Imports—of machine parts, trucks, diesel fuel and gasoline, infrastructure components for electricity and water systems, and food and medicines—had fallen sixty percent since the previous year. Agriculture had plummeted fifty percent with food rotting in fields from no gasoline for trucking to markets. Rodriguez predicted that the country would likely suffer "a famine causing hundreds of thousands of deaths within the next twelve months," mainly from the drop in oil production and sales due to Trump's 2017 and 2019 sanctions.

Adding fuel to then inferno, then-National Security Adviser John Bolton sabotaged ongoing talks taking place in Norway between President Maduro and the opposition. The preposterous statement–that Venezuela was causing a "national emergency" and was an "unusual and extraordinary threat to the national security of the United States"–has justified every executive order issued against Venezuela by Presidents Obama and Trump.

What possible threat could Venezuela—or Cuba, for decades—pose? Being socialist governments? Lifting their poorest out of abject poverty while we accelerate economic inequality? Housing the homeless better than the US? Achieving higher literacy rates in the case of both countries and longer life expectancy, in the case of socialist Cuba, than we have?

Our real national security threat is the erosion of democracy and morality within our borders when we cage Central American refugee children, terrorizing them and violating their human rights. We have a history of undermining and overturning democratically elected governments—Iran in 1953, Guatemala in 1954, El Salvador in 1960, Chile in 1973, Honduras in 2009, to name a few. Yet we hypocritically demonize other governments for endangering our national security.

As we starve those poorer brown and black-skinned Venezuelans who legally elected, as validated by the Carter Center and other monitors, and continue to support their current government, another vital sign of our political degradation is that both parties, Republican and Democrat with few low-voiced exceptions, support the *ongoing war by another name.*

Recall the Monroe Doctrine of 1823 from grade school history? President James Monroe proclaimed that European nations could not colonize nor otherwise interfere in North and South American countries. Ironically, since 1890, the US has intervened in Latin American elections, civil wars, and revolutions at least fifty-six times to bolster US corporate interests and to eliminate democratical-ly-elected governments and leftist movements, according to historian and author Mark Becker.

How true that *we have met the enemy and he is us*.

Originally published August 25, 2019 at *Common Dreams*. Reprinted with permission.

Refugees at the US-Mexican Border

We are here because you were there!

—slogan of the 1980 UK
immigrants' rights campaign

Why would so many Guatemalans, knowing the hatred likely to be heaped on them by the Trump Administration, have made the arduous journey to the US-Mexican border seeking refuge? A short list of our long history of corporate exploitation and military aggression in that country might explain.

Guatemala

In 1928, the American United Fruit Company, present-day Chiquita Banana International, instigated a massacre of thousands of Guatemalan workers who struck for better working conditions. Brigadier General Smedley Butler, who gained the highest rank and a host of medals for leading military interventions, popularly known as the Banana Wars in Central America and the Caribbean in the 1920s, put it bluntly. In his iconoclastic book *War Is a Racket*, he confessed, to having been "a bully boy for American corporations," by making countries safe for US capitalism.

In 1954 President Eisenhower ordered the overthrow of democratically elected President Jacobo Arbenz, who had issued the Agrarian Reform Law that redistributed land to some five-hundred-thousand landless, indigenous peasants. Ten years of democracy in that country from 1944 to 1954 was gutted, and the US installed an authoritarian government to roll back agrarian and worker reforms and, thus, protect United Fruit's land interests. Throughout the 1960s, 1970s, and 1980s Cold War era, the US backed coups and aided right-wing leaders with troops and weapons to repress left-leaning social movements, resulting in the deaths of hundreds of thousands of Guatemalans. One president we championed, Efrain Rios Montt, was convicted of genocide in 2013 for trying to eliminate Mayan peasants. The inequality and violence we have fostered and aided forced those Guatemalans—under attack, rendered landless, and impoverished—to leave and migrate north.

They are here because we were there.

Honduras

In 2009, reform-minded President Manuel Zelaya, who had raised minimum wage, built new schools, instituted school lunch programs, and provided pensions for the elderly, was kidnapped by the Honduran military and flown out of the country to Costa Rica. The general who led the coup was trained by the US Army at its School of the Americas, renamed Western Hemisphere Institute for Security Cooperation in 2001 and popularly known as the School of Assassins for the generous number of Latin American graduates who have instigated coups and tortured and murdered political opponents.

The Obama Administration tacitly supported the 2009 coup and had an assisting role in preventing Zelaya's return to Honduras. The US administration has continued to approve subsequent illegal Honduran presidents who have intimidated and violently suppressed rural and indigenous farmers' land rights in favor of large agro-corporate land grabs. Since 2011, the police, military, and hired militias have murdered thousands of indigenous activists, peasant leaders, journalists, human rights and union activists, opposition candidates, and judges. By 2016, Honduras had the highest murder rate in the world.

Drug traffickers have infiltrated the Honduran government "from top to bottom," including the police and military, according to Dana Frank, historian, activist, and author of *The Long Honduran Night*. The brother of the president, whom we backed and supported with US aid, was charged in 2019 in the US with trafficking multi tons of cocaine headed to the US and sentenced to life in prison. He was assisted by national police also funded by the US and drug traffickers.

Meanwhile, US Border Patrol agents tear-gassed Honduran asylum seekers fleeing police, drug-gang violence, and the loss of their land due to the climate crisis. The border patrol separated thousands of Central American children from their families and dumped them into cold, crowded detention centers with filthy toilets and insufficient running water.

They are here because we were there.

El Salvador

Over the past eight decades, US military support for right-wing coups and authoritarian candidates has strangled social movements for self-determination, worker rights, and economic development in El Salvador. In 1932, the US and Britain, owners of large export-oriented coffee plantations, sent naval support to quell a peasant rebellion led by the Marxist-Leninist Farabundo Marti.

In 1960, President Dwight D. Eisenhower, fearing a leftist government, facilitated a right-wing coup and openly opposed the holding of free elections in El Salvador. The same Cold War ideology drove President Ronald Reagan to provide generous military assistance and training in 1983 to the repressive military-led government in its civil war against a leftist front. Eighty thousand Salvadorans were killed in the 1980-1992 civil war, with the majority of civilian deaths caused by Salvadoran military and death squads. In the early 1990s some two hundred thousand Salvadorans were given Temporary Protected Status. However, their TPS was revoked in 2018 by President Donald J. Trump, emblematic of his hostile and hate-mongering history toward the poor, displaced, and endangered *who arrive here because we were there.*

Originally published July 17, 2019 in the *Berkshire Eagle*. Reprinted with permission.

Agent Orange: The Unfinished War in Vietnam

President Bill Clinton announced in 1995 that the United States was resuming diplomatic relations with Vietnam and, thus, ending our postwar trade embargo and a suite of punishing maneuvers that cut Vietnam off from international aid and economic development. The period of starving Vietnam economically after our failure to defeat them militarily has been characterized as the second American War in Vietnam.

The diplomatic opening to Vietnam followed on the heels of a domestic decision made in 1991, namely to give health-related care and disability benefits to US veterans whose children suffered a select set of illnesses and birth defects associated with their parents' service in the US war in Vietnam.

For nearly twenty years after the war's end in April 1975, the United States Department of Veterans Affairs or VA and other related parts of government had treated veterans of that politically fraught war as pariahs, blaming their illnesses on drugs, alcohol, PTSD—everything but the chemical warfare we conducted in Vietnam from 1961 to 1971. Further, the VA held Vietnam veterans to a more rigorous standard of proof for disability than veterans of previous wars.

Veterans won some meager justice only through organizing national networks, public protests, press conferences, and legal challenges against chemical companies that manufactured Agent Orange and the government, which approved its use. Ultimately, it was the support of Congress in passing the Agent Orange Act of 1991 that won some lasting justice in medical treatment and disability for Vietnam veterans.

If our veterans were treated so callously by our government, what of the Vietnamese victims of Agent Orange?

During the ten years from 1961 to 1971 of aerial chemical warfare in Vietnam, US warplanes sprayed more than twenty-million gallons of herbicide defoliants, chief among them Agent Orange, named for the orange stripe on its fifty-five-gallon container. The defoliant was used to destroy the Vietnamese forest cover and food crops of National Liberation Front forces, pejoratively named Viet Cong.

By 1965, Agent Orange was sprayed on populated Vietnamese villages in increased volumes. Extensive loss of forest cover, rubber plantations, mangroves, wildlife, crops, animals, and freshwater fish ensued. Rural midwives and urban obstetricians began reporting newborns with animal-like faces and hydrocephalic heads, missing limbs, missing facial parts, conjoined twins, and many other deformities, all likely attributable to Agent Orange.

In 1968, a young obstetrician in Saigon's Tu Du Hospital, Dr. Nguyen Thi Ngoc Phuong, reported delivering grossly deformed fetuses and infants with increasing frequency, some so horrific she could not show them to their parents. Given the denial on the part of the South Vietnam and US governments about the negative health effects of Agent Orange, she preserved dozens of deformed fetuses in formaldehyde. They remain today as chilling evidence of the teratogenic effects—embryonic or fetal effects—of Agent Orange.

Dr. Phuong created a residential nursery and home in Tu Du Hospital for handicapped babies whose parents lacked resources and capacity to care for them at home. The Tu Du Hospital Peace Village, as it is called, has sheltered, provided medical and rehabilitative services, raised, and educated hundreds of Agent Orange victims.

Agent Orange was also truck- and hand-sprayed to clear vegetation around US military bases. Former US pilots later disclosed that they dumped hundreds of thousands of gallons from their planes into forests, rivers, and drinking-water reservoirs because military regulations required that herbicide-spray planes return to base empty. In that methodical ecocide, up to one-fourth of South Vietnam was sprayed, and nearly one-half of coastal mangrove forests—nurseries for marine life that fed South Vietnam—were destroyed. By the end of the war, an estimated five million Vietnamese had been exposed to Agent Orange, an exposure which has resulted in "four-hundred-thousand deaths and disabilities and a half million children born with birth defects," according to the 2008-2009 President's Cancer Panel Report.

Today a third and fourth generation of children born with horrific birth defects and mental retardation continue to suffer the legacy of our chemical warfare in Vietnam.

Why ongoing toxicity after decades of the war's end? The best studies to date have found that the extremely virulent strain of dioxin in Agent Orange, known as TCDD, persists in the environment of

Vietnam, particularly in areas most heavily sprayed and on former US air bases where Agent Orange was stored, loaded into spraying equipment, spilled, and also used liberally to clear the periphery of the bases. Washed into local ponds during tropical rainstorms, dioxin in pond sediment is long-lived and bioaccumulates in the food chain, contaminating the fish, duck, and freshwater mollusks harvested by people living on or near the former bases.

Recent studies by the Canadian firm Hatfield Associates found that levels of dioxin in breast milk of women living on former US bases greatly exceed World Health Organization standards for breastfeeding infants. That dioxin, as ongoing research has found, is a carcinogen, a teratogen resulting in birth defects, and an endocrine-disrupting compound, with the potential to damage the functions of the body's entire hormone system.

Did the federal government, Monsanto, Dow Chemical, Diamond Shamrock, and other manufacturers of Agent Orange know about its human toxicity?

Investigations of court and US National Archives documents have uncovered that Dow Chemical Company learned as early as 1965 and possibly 1955 from a German manufacturer that the dioxin contaminant in Agent Orange, TCDD, is "one of the most toxic materials known causing not only skin lesions but also liver damage."

In 1965, Dow wrote a confidential memo to other manufacturers regarding the exceptionally toxic dioxin in Agent Orange and expressed concern about government regulating and limiting production—and thus profits—if the information went public. In turn, the US government consistently claimed ignorance about the human-toxicity potential of Agent Orange throughout the 1970s and 1980s. However, in 1988, a conscience-stricken former senior scientist at the US Air Force Chemical Weapons Branch, Dr. James Clary, put into writing this incriminatory statement:

> When we initiated the herbicide program in the 1960s, we were aware of the potential for damage due to dioxin contamination in the herbicide. We were even aware that the military formulation had a higher dioxin concentration than the civilian version due to the lower cost and speed of manufacture. However, because the material was to be used on the enemy, none of us were

overly concerned. We never considered a scenario in which our own personnel would become contaminated with the herbicide.

Even in the face of new evidence, neither the industries nor the government will acknowledge what they knew about Agent Orange toxicity at the time of its manufacture and use. Both take cover behind the callous claim that there is no adequate scientific evidence proving adverse health effects in war veterans from Agent Orange/dioxin exposure: limited evidence, suggestive evidence, and statistical correlation at best, but not definitive proof.

Further, the industries are handily protected by the government-contractor-immunity clause. In retrospect, both the industries and government sinned by omission. They failed to conduct rigorous human health studies on workers exposed occupationally and on exposed veterans during and after the war because they did not want to face the potential consequences.

Journey through Vietnam

In March of 2014, I traveled through Vietnam from Hanoi to Da Nang in central Vietnam to Ho Chi Minh City, formerly Saigon. The purpose of my journey was to investigate the plight of third- and fourth-generation Agent Orange dioxin victims, the fate of dioxin-contaminated sites, the extent of ecological restoration needed, and what is being done to overcome those wounds of war.

I visited models of community-based care for Agent Orange victims that rival our best ones for disabled children and staffed by people who spoke of the children they cared for as their family. I found that those working to rid Agent Orange from Vietnam's environment harbor no antipathy toward American citizens even as they clamor for justice from the United States government to pay for the health and environmental costs from our ten years of chemical warfare.

If President Richard Nixon's 1973 peace negotiations' pledge of $3.25 billion for reconstruction—a pledge spurned by Presidents Ford and Carter and rejected by Congress—were honored in today's dollars, the inflation-adjusted pledge of more than $21.5 billion would support all the costs of health, housing, and educational services for Agent Orange victims. It would also support ecological restoration of forests and mangroves and some remediation costs of

*The Ho Chi Minh City Peace Village Team includes, from left,
Major General Tran Ngoc Tho, director; Dr. Nguyen Thi Phuong Tan,
chief of the rehabilitation department, Tu Du Hospital; an unidentified
peace village student translator; an unidentified staff member;
author Pat Hynes; Dang Hong Nhut, peace village vice-president*

photo courtesy of Ho Chi Minh City Peace Village

remaining dioxin hotspots.

More than a dozen designated Peace Villages, some with organic gardens, orchards, and animals, have been built for children and, in some cases, for Vietnamese veterans who have severe mental and/or physical challenges. Children of Peace Villages receive rehabilitative care and physical therapy, and those able to learn are prepared for higher education or taught vocational skills such as sewing, flower-making, fabricating incense sticks, and more to help support themselves and their families. Hundreds more Peace Villages are needed for the estimated tens of thousands of multigenerational victims.

Peace Villages are organized and built by the Vietnam Association for Victims of Agent Orange, VAVA, with funds from the Vietnam government and international supporters. Many staff and administrators are retired Vietnamese war veterans, and some staff are themselves physically handicapped from their parents' exposure to

Agent Orange. Some pioneers in the effort to undo the ongoing harm of the Vietnam War and heal their own spiritual wounds of war are American veterans who raise funds for the Peace Villages, volunteer their services, and bring other veterans in the spirit of reconciliation.

When I asked about their striking commitment to the Peace Villages, retired Vietnamese veterans spoke of having lost so many friends in the war that, having lived, they want to give back to war victims. One former general likened his iron-willed commitment to his country's two-thousand-year-old history of success against invaders and colonizers. "We beat the Chinese," he said. "We beat the French. We beat the Americans. Now I want to beat Agent Orange."

A young university student working in the VAVA Ho Chi Minh City office said quietly, "Look at me," pointing to his head shaped like a light bulb. "I hope my passion will contribute to other Agent Orange victims' happiness and freedom."

A medical doctor responsible for rehabilitative care of children at the Tu Du Hospital Peace Village responded, "My life is bound to the Agent-Orange babies, and I am passionate about their right to be treated humanely."

Like many US visitors to Vietnam before me, I found in Vietnam a people forward-looking and forgiving, a poor country—rendered more so by the twenty-five-year US embargo which ended in 2000—doggedly lifting itself out of poverty, and a country determined not to leave behind their victims of Agent Orange.

Perhaps most telling of their spirit is the response of a Vietnamese veteran when asked by US veteran James Zumwalt why Vietnamese are not bitter towards Americans. "We Vietnamese have small bodies," he replied. "If we fill them with hate, there is no room for love," a well of wisdom from which we Americans could draw.

Originally published in Published in *Z Magazine* October 26, 2015.,

Partnerships

Returning from Vietnam, I resolved to inform Americans of the ongoing legacy of the US War in Vietnam and our responsibility and opportunities for undoing its legacy. In support of the Peace Villages, the Traprock Center for Peace and Justice created the Vietnam Peace Village Fund and, through many public presentations, we raised

*A teacher among moringa trees
with students of Nham School*

photo copyright by Phung Tuu Boi

money to support thirty annual scholarships to Peace Villages for third and fourth generation child victims of Agent Orange.

Unable to visit a prominent tree-planting project in a rural part of Vietnam, I corresponded with its founder, the Vietnamese botanist Phung Tuu Boi and his organization, the Nature Conservation and Community Development Center. He sent photos and the history of their work in Dong Son commune, located in A Loui Valley of North Central Vietnam once heavily bombed and sprayed with herbicide during the US war in Vietnam. Dong Son is known as a dioxin hotspot and remains one of the poorest villages in the valley with fifty percent of its population living below Vietnam's poverty line.

Staff of the Nature Conservation and Community Development Center work with residents of Dong Son to plant trees and seedlings. They have introduced residents and the local kindergarten staff to the moringa tree, called the miracle tree for its health benefits, and staff have also provided them with seedlings and assisted in planting the trees. The kindergarten serves children nutritious moringa soup from its own trees. Villagers are also supported in creating their own nurseries in order to promote economic empowerment, restore biodiversity, enhance community nutrition, and mitigate climate change.

Phung Tuu Boi's committed work inspired a partnership we called 10,000 Trees for Vietnam. Through public presentations, an exhibit and sale of Andy Rothschild's sculptures of recycled materials at Greenfield's Artspace Community Art Center, the ongoing generosity of the Voluntary Carbon Tax Witness of Leverett's Mount Toby Friends Meeting, and contributions from other loyal benefactors, Traprock has raised more than sixteen thousand dollars for tree nurseries and planting moringa trees in Vietnam.

Traprock Center Helping Young People Build a Better World through Books

by Richie Davis

I am grateful to Richie Davis, a well-loved writer and editor for the *Greenfield Recorder*, for responding to my request that he write the following article on the children's books collaboration between the Traprock Center for Peace and Justice and Women's International League for Peace and Freedom, WILPF, Sierra Leone.

Since 2019, Traprock has supported and collaborated with WILPF Sierra Leone on their Sports for Peace project for teen athletes in four local schools, their 2020-2021 COVID Education and Prevention Project, and most recently, their Respect for Girls initiative to confront the sexual harassment of girls in schools by teachers. Respect for Girls is an ongoing collaboration between Sarah Pirtle's Long Line for Racial Justice and WILPF Sierra Leone youth members.

—Pat Hynes

Like the one thousand paper cranes folded to commemorate the prayers of Hiroshima children for peace, the one hundred paperback books flying into the hands of young readers in West Africa mark a conviction by Traprock Center for Peace and Justice that young people can help build a better world.

The books, with titles like *I Have a Dream, Wangari's Trees for Peace*, and *I Am Malala* are greeting students at two schools in Freetown, Sierra Leone, after Traprock board member Pat Hynes met Kadie Sesay, president of Women's International League for Peace and Freedom Sierra Leone in August 2018 at the African Women's Feminist Peace Conference.

Traprock's Children's Books Collaborative—which has already placed a hundred books about peace and justice in public libraries in Greenfield, Turners Falls, and Orange—caught the attention of Sesay, a former schoolteacher in the West African country. She suggested to Hynes a collaboration with the American organization to get similar books into schools in her country.

Hynes, who's found test-focused teaching an impediment in getting schools here to accept Traprock's grants for books with themes of social justice, peace, and the environment, welcomed the opportunity to introduce them in a country where equality for women, fostering democracy, and lifting the country out of poverty are all key issues.

The degree of women's equality in a country, Hynes says, is the best predictor of how peaceful or conflict-ridden that country is, according to WomanStats studies of 175 countries. She stresses the importance of encouraging young people to help promote gender equality.

Hynes, a member of Women's International League for Peace and Freedom, convinced the global organization's Boston chapter

School children receive Children's Collaborative books,
in Freetown, Sierra Leone
photo copyright by Peter Alfred

to contribute toward helping the Sierra Leonian chapter acquire computer equipment and other support to help in its work.

It might seem that reading Nicola Davies's *The Lion Who Stole My Arm* or *I am Malala*—about the Nobel-winning teen who advocated for educating girls in Afghanistan—wouldn't do much to save a world where democracies are threatened and the dangers of climate change are ignored. Planting seeds for grassroots community resources to encourage peace also represents a departure from the kinds of citizen demonstrations Traprock was best known for in the 1970s and 1980s.

But Hynes sees ways the book project—like Traprock's twenty-five-year-old Journey Camp for girls and its Young Peacemakers Awards—can inspire young people to "dream behind their horizons," in her words. It can open their minds to role models fostering diversity and conflict resolution.

In Sierra Leone, where female genital mutilation persists and there are ongoing efforts to recover from the effects of a decade-long 1990s Blood Diamond civil war that left more than 120,000 dead and millions of refugees following mass brutality by children soldiers, the collaborative book project also offers hope, Sesay believes.

Hynes and Sesay hope the African children, ages from four to sixteen and including more than 650 high school students, can become ambassadors for conflict resolution and environmental stewardship to encourage peers as well as adults "in the community and beyond" to follow the examples of Malala Yousafzai, Martin Luther King Jr., and Kenyan Nobel Prize-winning environmentalist Wangari Maathai, among others.

There are also tree-planting and other environmental education projects planned as part of a broader community outreach.

By finding relevant role models for children, Hynes says, Traprock hopes the books with broad international themes of diversity and equality can empower young people to become active players in restoring democracy, resolving conflict, and fighting income inequality within their societies.

"Books can affect young people in ways to inspire, to dream beyond their horizons," she says. Especially if they're read in a classroom or another group setting with a teacher or parent to help them interpret the lessons, she believes, books can serve to enlighten young readers—in our communities as well as in other countries—to move toward a more peaceful future.

Richie Davis was a writer and editor for more than forty years at *Greenfield Recorder*. The retired senior writer at *Greenfield Recorder* in Massachusetts, he earned more than thirty-five regional news and feature-writing awards during a career of more than forty years. He blogs at RichieDavis.net and is author of *Inner Landscapes: True Tales from Extraordinary Lives* and *Good Will & Ice Cream: More True Tales from Extraordinary Lives.*

Originally published September 8, 2019 in the *Greenfield Recorder*. Reprinted with permission.

COVID-19

The COVID-19 virus pandemic is an unparalleled health crisis in our lifetime. Worse, it converged in 2020 with record-shattering climate crises, including extreme forest fires in the US West that consumed four percent of California land and an immense hurricane season in the Caribbean and the Gulf of Mexico. Concurrently, our country was riven with political polarization and potential civil war-like unrest during and after the 2020 US presidential election.

In a vacuum of federal leadership and science-denial, COVID ran out of control in the United States—*otherwise deemed the medical mecca of the world*—with 14.4 million infections and 252,373 deaths by early December 2020. We are 4% of the world's population, yet we had 18.3% of the world's deaths by late 2020.

Of all who died from COVID by October 2020, it was estimated that more than a hundred thousand had unnecessarily lost their lives because of President Trump's malevolent negligence as he abandoned disease control and left it to the states. Worse, half of those who lost their lives from the tragedy of COVID are the same second-class citizens who are multiply harmed across their lives by poverty, racism, and environmental pollution. By late August 2020, the Associated Press reported that fifty percent of all COVID deaths in the US were people of color–Blacks, Hispanics, Native Americans, and Asian Americans—while they constitute just less than forty percent of our population.

Further, had the US followed public health guidelines for stemming infection rates as did other wealthy industrial countries, by October "nearly nine million more people would have been employed." And who were the majority unemployed? The coronavirus recession has eliminated low-wage mainly service jobs at an estimated eight times the rate of high wage jobs, harming most Black workers, Hispanic men, those without college degrees, and mothers with children, according to a *Washington Post* analysis. This profile of deepened poverty stands in stark contrast to the middle and upper middle classes and the wealthy: by the end of summer 2020, white-collar jobs, housing value, and the stock market had mostly recovered.

One shaft of light during the ongoing perfect storm is the extraordinary commitment and integrity of medical, educational, food, and other essential workers within workplaces ill-prepared or caught by surprise. In parallel, innumerable kindnesses of neighbors and volunteers—making masks for others when they were scarce, shopping and delivering meals to the poor and homebound, helping others with overdue bills, organizing summer concerts with social distancing on porches—manifest that the golden rule survives the Trump administration's soulless dismissal of public health measures for stemming the epidemic. "They are the antibodies to indifference," to borrow Pope Francis' words.

A low-spirit and anxious mood infected many, variously regarding adequate education for their children, economic recovery for the millions of jobless running out of unemployment insurance, and social isolation. A few health equity experts presciently identified that we need equally a "social vaccine" together with an effective medical vaccine to emerge from the global crisis *as a better world* rather than one of greater inequality and conflict. The social vaccine would engender a life of reliable social protections for everyone—a habitable planet that sustains biodiversity, government that governs for all with strong citizen participation, and a spirit of partnership among governments in a multilateral world delivered from militarized "Great-Power" competition.

A pipedream? No. We need a global Green New Deal with universal commitment akin to the creation of the United Nations after the acute global conflict and genocide of World War II.

What of a Gender New Deal? COVID exposed a pandemic within the pandemic—violence against women in the home increased here and globally during COVID. Further, experts who study masculinity and public health contend that many men perceive wearing masks and practicing social distancing as "unmanly" and appearing weak—at a "destructive cost" to themselves and those around them.

The five following COVID dispatches span May through December 2020. COVID-19 vaccines projected for 2021-2022 will hopefully end the medical pandemic. Only a social vaccine will cure the other ills—social, economic, environmental, political and militaristic—of our society and world.

On December 8, 2020, the House of Representatives passed a bipartisan veto-proof defense budget bill of $740 billion for 2021 while the months-old, downsized COVID relief bill languished in Congress. A social vaccine would expose and expunge the "moral rot at the center of US politics . . . that we can find the money for war but not for corona virus relief."

By June 17, 2021, thanks to the Biden Administration prioritizing COVID vaccination, sixty-five percent of US adults were at least partially vaccinated.

How then does a pandemic manifest inequality?

With the greatest total wealth of any country, the United States had the highest number of confirmed coronavirus cases and deaths of any country in the world as of September 2021, higher at the time than countries with four times as many people, namely China and India, a relatively poor country. Our failure in public and medical health was worsened by a callous, *know-nothing* president who underfunded federal health agencies, disbanded pandemic expert teams, refused to respect the basic rudiments of science, and cared more about the fallout of COVID-19 on the upcoming election and his faltering poll numbers than his citizens.

Who are, then, the most likely victims of the virus? Workers of color, both black Americans and Latinos, are proportionately found in the lowest-paying service and domestic occupations. Two thirds of those workers are women. That means more exposure to risk-laden work in many cases—agricultural workers and those in meat processing, hospitals and nursing homes, and janitorial and housekeeping in health care facilities. They are more likely to plunge into deeper poverty if infected, laid off without health insurance or paid sick leave. They cannot "stay in place" working from home online as the professional class can. Further, Blacks and Latinos are more likely to live in environmental injustice communities, meaning they are more frequently exposed to air and water pollution and toxic wastes than whites. Harvard-based research found that those exposed to greater air pollution from cars and factories are more vulnerable to contracting COVID-19.

Add to economic and environmental inequality the social inequality of racial discrimination—in hiring, in pay, in "driving while Black," in persistent housing segregation, in greater rates of arrests and prison terms, in day-to-day interpersonal exclusion and slights inducing unrelenting stress—and we find reasons for higher rates of COVID-19 infections and deaths among Latinos and Blacks.

In New York, for example, African Americans were twice as likely to die from COVID-19 as white people. As of mid April, 2020 counties with a majority of African Americans had three times the infection rates as counties with a white majority. Chelsea, Massachusetts, long a working class city with a majority of Latinos and immense daily air polluting traffic to Boston crossing the Tobin Bridge overhead, was the hotspot of infections in Massachusetts.

No, COVID-19 is not the great equalizer. If anything, it exposed the fault line of injustice that runs through this country, wherein:

- the wealthy can "shelter in place" on gigantic yachts
- wealthier private and non-profit hospitals hold much larger cash reserves than safety-net hospitals for the poor and uninsured
- larger businesses get preference over smaller ones for government loans
- the professional class can work from home with their children having access to computers for online learning, and
- corporate insurance and pharmaceutical companies lobby against a single-payer health care system

We urgently need health care for all *and* a working social democracy.

Originally published May 19, 2020 in the *Greenfield Recorder*. Reprinted with permission.

Women Rise to Heroic Heights During COVID-19
from the perspective of May, 2020

Women have risen to heroic heights during the pandemic as they comprise the majority of essential health care workers, lead countries successful in containing the coronavirus, and homeschooling children while working from home. And yet, the global pandemic in physical and sexual violence against women continues unabated and has worsened during the coronavirus pandemic.

Heroic Heights

As of mid-April 2020, women led six of seven countries with the best records of containing COVID-19 infections and deaths: Germany, Taiwan, New Zealand, Iceland, Finland, Norway, and Denmark. While most of those frontrunners are small, Germany is the most populous country in Western Europe. And Norway is comparable in population to medical mecca Massachusetts, which became a hotspot of infection and deaths soon after New York City, given its delay in implementing a testing- and contact-tracing program.

Though taking different approaches, some with lockdowns, some without, women-led successful countries acted immediately and decisively with testing, tracking, widespread education, adequate personal protection, and ongoing personal communication through press conferences, some for children only. Remarking on the example of those women leaders, one commentator—a consultant to businesses on women's leadership—points to studies that show "women are more likely to lead through inspiration, transforming people's attitudes and beliefs, and aligning people with meaning and purpose than men are."

Nurses 9% Male and 91% Female on the Front Lines

The crisp crisis-driven prose of Simone Hannah-Clark, an intensive-care-unit nurse in New York City, takes us non-stop through one long day typical of those experienced by the hundreds of thousands of critical care nurses on the front lines of the pandemic:

- rising early while her family slept
- avoiding the too quiet, dark subway (because of risk of sexual assault?) in favor of Lyft

- at the hospital having to quickly wedge two beds, ventilators and sets of monitors into rooms sized for one, for the tidal wave of COVID-19 patients
- swiftly hooking up her patients to a half dozen monitors and machines
- haunted with worry about reusing personal protective equipment in short supply throughout a 12-hour shift, and
- bearing respectful witness to those who die

"We wrap the patient's body, securely, stroking her brow and wishing her well on her next journey."

"Doctors," she continued, "may be the architects of what happens in the hospital. But we are the builders."

And so the nurses—ninety-one percent women—build ceaselessly amidst overflowing trash buckets and shortages of equipment, sedating drugs, stretchers, and beds within the chaos of a broken health care system.

Cook County Hospital, Chicago's safety net and largest hospital, serves the poor, homeless, incarcerated, insured and uninsured, immigrants regardless of legal status, and mainly people of color. An emergency room nurse there recounts the tactic she resorted to in order to get N-95 masks and other personal protective equipment, PPE, for the ER nurses assisting extremely ill COVID-19 patients: *a work sit-down* in the break room. The ER coordinator immediately found a PPE cart and N-95 masks for the nurses—*equipment readily available to ER doctors*—but wasted no time in demeaning their action as a "temper tantrum."

"Something management would say only to nurses, who are between eighty and ninety percent women . . . ," the nurse notes. To which she adds, "We are fighting back daily on the inside."

As of May 12, 2020, ninety-one US nurses had died from COVID-19 while none had died in Canada, where a national-ized health care system prioritizes people over profit, meaning no Canadian nurses have to resort to using garbage bags and work sit-downs for personal protection. Canada has one-tenth the population of the US.

The Underbelly of "Shelter in Place"

Home, the refuge from the coronavirus, is the hot spot for physical and sexual assault of women and children. Almost one in three women throughout the world aged fifteen and over have experienced physical and/or sexual intimate-partner violence during their lifetime. Violence by an intimate partner is the leading cause of injury to women between fifteen and forty-four years old.

This relentless pandemic in violence is magnified with women having to stay in place with their batterers to protect against COVID-19. As one feminist activist states, "this coronavirus pandemic can trigger a wave of violence committed by men unable [*and unwilling*, I would add] to deal with the psychological, financial, and social consequences of the crisis."

The ER for assaulted women includes hotlines, shelters, the courts, and hospitals—all needed but deeply inadequate without systemic prevention of assault. We—parents, educators, relatives and friends, media, religious leaders, politicians, coaches, and mentors at large—must challenge boys and men to be "another boy, another man against violence against women." Above all, men and boys must take responsibility for their emancipation from toxic male identity and behavior in seeking a path to healthy manhood.

Originally published May 20, 2020 at *Common Dreams*. Reprinted with permission.

A Pandemic within the Pandemic

On March 23, 2020, as COVID-19 was overtaking the world, United Nations Secretary General Antonio Guterres pleaded for peace:

> To warring parties—
>
> Pull back from hostilities. Silence the guns. Stop the artillery.
>
> End the airstrikes . . . End the sickness of war and fight the disease that is ravaging our world. It starts by stopping the fighting everywhere. Now. That is what our human family needs, now more than ever.

Two weeks later, horrified by the global surge in male violence against women, he again implored for peace:

Peace is not just the absence of war. Many women under lockdown for COVID-19 face violence where they should be safest—in their own homes. Today I appeal for peace in homes around the world. I urge all governments to put women's safety first as they respond to the pandemic.

In every region of the world, battery and sexual assault of women and girls isolated at home increased with the spread of the coronavirus. Reports from China's Hubei province indicated that domestic violence tripled during February 2020 compared to February 2019. In France, violence against women increased thirty percent after the country initiated a March 17, 2020, lockdown, in Argentina by twenty-five percent, and in Singapore by thirty-three percent. The pandemic in sexual assault of women and girls followed the COVID-19 pandemic in what Executive Director of UN Women Phumzile Mlambo-Ngcuka called "a perfect storm for violent behavior behind closed doors." By the end of May 2020, nearly 250 million women and girls had reported suffering sexual or physical violence by an intimate partner, *a far greater number than those infected by the virus.*

"Stay Safe—Stay Home" is one of the essential public health measures in containing the COVID virus. Yet home is a dangerous and unsafe place for those one-in-three women worldwide who are physically and/or sexually abused or stalked over their lifetime, most by a male relative or intimate partner at home. Further, intimate partners commit one half of femicides—the killing of women *because they are women*—throughout the world. School, the workplace, outdoors—anywhere is safer than home for women and girls at risk of domestic violence.

An estimated 1.6 billion of the world's children lost their in-school education because of COVID-19, with many in developing countries lacking the benefit of online education at home. For girls, that setback can be yet more dangerous, more violent, and more life-limiting. Boarding schools in Tanzania have saved girls from female genital mutilation until COVID sent them home. According to the non-governmental organization Terre des Hommes, which runs a safe house for girls, "The community has taken advantage of this situation of COVID-19 and where children are now back at home, they are cutting their girls. They know it is against the law, but they are not afraid."

During the 2014-2016 Ebola crisis in Africa, many children were kept out of school at home, especially girls, according to Eric Hazard of Save the Children. "Over eleven thousand girls in Sierra Leone became pregnant," due to sexual violence and abuse.

Given that the same is assuredly occurring now with our current pandemic, what recourse to health care do women and girls have? Some governments in COVID lockdown did not classify sexual and reproductive health—for pregnancy, childbirth, abortion, and birth control—as essential, forcing the health centers to close. In the case of India, the institutions were repurposed for COVID. The UN Population Fund Director Natalia Kanen calls the effect of COVID–19 on women and girls "devastating" given estimates of seven million unintended pregnancies worldwide and potentially thousands of deaths from birth complications and unsafe abortions.

What of the situation in the United States? Crime rates declined in cities and counties across the US over the second half of March 2020—with one exception, *domestic violence*— as mandatory stay-at-home orders drove millions of residents to stay inside their homes. Calls by victims of domestic violence surged between ten and thirty percent, according to an analysis of crime data published by fifty-three law enforcement agencies in two dozen states.

Another more nuanced study found that the crimes that have dropped are more minor, younger peer-group crimes such as vandalism, car theft, and driving under the influence. The graver crimes of homicide and aggravated assault have remained the same. *Only intimate partner violence has increased.*

And what of the fate of women's reproductive health clinics? Twelve states quickly banned or blocked abortion services in response to the COVID-19 pandemic, justifying their actions by defining abortion services a non-essential health service. Many defended their actions under the aegis of conserving personal protective equipment. In response, the leading medical professional organizations, among them the American College of Obstetricians and Gynecologists, issued a public statement defining abortion as "an essential component of comprehensive health care."

Ultimately the bans were rescinded after successful court challenges or state executive action. However, in the time it took, many reproductive health clinics closed for financial reasons, and the consequences for women and girls in need of abortion, before the bans were lifted, are unknown.

But ending the stay-at-home order won't end violence against women. On average, at least one in three women in the US is beaten, coerced into sex, or otherwise abused by an intimate partner in the course of her lifetime.

More than one in three women regularly fears being sexually assaulted, according to a new report from Gallup. Violence against women is the "most common but least punished crime in the world," according to the UN, and it is a catastrophic obstacle for achieving women's equality worldwide.

As with systemic racism, we must as a society excavate and eliminate the structural roots of violence against women and girls: namely female inequality, rape culture, and the failure to treat violence against women as a serious offense.

Peace on earth begins with peace at home. The degree of equality women have within their families and in their society predicts best how peaceful or conflict-ridden their country is.

Originally published September 7, 2020, at *Portside*. Reprinted with permission.

Solving Dual Crises of COVID-19 and Climate Change

We are living with two life-threatening crises: COVID-19 and climate breakdown. They pose a common stark fate for us—the risk of illness in the case of COVID and injury and destruction of our environment in the case of climate. Both are harbingers of death for many. But their equally stark differences and our response as a world matter most for survival.

Countries that acted quickly against COVID and with strict restrictions, which kept most residents at home, were successful in keeping their death rates lower and slowing the virus spread by "flattening the curve" than countries with looser restrictions and those that waited to act. A recent study found "if cities across the US had moved just one week faster to shut down restaurants and businesses and require residents to stay at home, they could have avoided thirty-five thousand coronavirus deaths by early May 2020." If they had acted two weeks earlier, "more than fifty thousand people who died from the pandemic might be alive."

There is, however, no flattening of the global emissions curve or of global temperature rise despite successive UN climate conference agreements. We are on a course to crash past emissions targets set by the 2015 Paris Climate Agreement. The recent plummet in global carbon dioxide emissions from the COVID-induced economic slowdown is *incidental* not intentional. Further, the Trump administration—in diabolic denial of science, facts, and truth—spurned the 2015 agreement, weakened our environmental regulations, and coddled the nearly bankrupt fossil-fuel industry with COVID recovery funds.

Unlike COVID, no one country or city can save itself from the global climate crisis, even with emergency plans and equipment. Turning back from the perilous path of unchecked global warming and biodiversity loss requires global cohesiveness and a massive cooperative effort among all countries, especially the largest, most industrialized, most consuming, and most militarized. Unchecked global warming and the accelerated loss in biodiversity could collapse whole ecosystems within ten years, according to the most recent climate science. Ten years of action, beginning now, to aggressively slow the climate crisis, is akin to having acted one week sooner to stem the pandemic.

At the pace of deforestation in the Amazon for cattle farming and resource extraction, the rainforest is moving from capturing and storing the greenhouse gas carbon dioxide to releasing more than it removes. The same pattern is occurring in Central African rainforests. Virtually every threat to biological life on earth being studied is revealing an accelerated pace of loss: massive death of coral reefs, which support twenty-five percent of marine life, from faster warming oceans while more destructive monster storms with winds over 155 miles per hour have increased since the 1980s, especially in the southeastern US and the Caribbean. We are nearing threshold temperatures that will melt most of the Greenland and West Antarctica ice shelves and the Arctic sea ice, presaging slow, long-term sea-level rise that will threaten the world's coastal cities—none spared. A decade of studies reinforces that the American West and Southwest are moving inexorably toward desert with record-breaking drought, tree death, and wildfire.

The COVID-19 crisis was immediate and stark, and many, if not most, countries acted successfully in their own deserved self-interest. An exceptional Cuba acted also in solidarity with others by offering generous medical assistance to a stranded cruise ship and countries in need. But the climate crisis, which has never been covered by the media with the intensity and non-stop reporting dedicated to COVID, will be far worse in the not-so-long term. The climate crisis will end up killing an estimated 250,000 people per year within two decades if little is done and potentially causing up to a billion climate migrants within three decades, according to the UN, if the world does not act now and aggressively.

How to turn the climate crisis into a fragment of opportunity? Recover and rebuild the economy, which may take ten years, with the goal of replacing fossil fuels with renewable energy and intensive efficiency.

How to finance?

- eliminate hundred-year-old subsidies to the fossil fuel industries, which in turn would save billions of dollars in health costs from their pollution
- end the costly naval defense of Persian Gulf oil. All together those actions would save an estimated $650 million dollars per year
- re-route the more than a trillion dollars committed to new nuclear weapons production and the technically skilled jobs to the green energy sector
- reduce substantially the nearly $750 billion dollar war and arms budget and re-invest the funds and arms industry jobs into the Green New Deal infrastructure

* leave existing natural forests untouched, and
* listen to and support youth climate activists

The European Commission has released a green economic recovery plan. Why not us also?

Originally published June 3, 2020 in the *Greenfield Recorder*. Reprinted with permission.

COVID and the Military

On May 18, 2020 the US Department of Veterans Affairs launched a Salvation Army-like charity drive asking the public for donations of money, food, and mobile phones to help an estimated forty thousand homeless veterans during the pandemic. More than half of all homeless veterans are African American and Hispanic while they account for only fifteen percent of US veterans, another punishing consequence of pervasive racism.

How is it that a country that spends nearly a trillion dollars each year on the military, national security, cybersecurity, and weapons manufacture—a country that touts itself as the military superpower of the world with soldiers and weapons on every continent except Antarctica—needs charity for its veterans?

The final end for World War II veterans at the Soldiers' Home in Holyoke, Massachusetts tragically mirrored their wartime experiences. Feted when first built in 1952, the Soldiers' Home has suffered serious shortages of protective gear during COVID and has been chronically underfunded and understaffed, such that the administrator combined wards of uninfected and infected men. Of 210 veterans living there, eighty-one had died by late May 2020—among the highest death tolls of any end-of-life facility in the country.

In late March 2020, Captain Brett Crozier sent an email up his chain of command regarding the hazardous conditions for the forty-eight-hundred crew members aboard the tightly-quartered aircraft carrier, USS *Theodore Roosevelt*, on which cases of coronavirus were growing. "We are not at war. Sailors do not need to die," he wrote. "If we do not act now, we are failing to properly take care of our most trusted asset—our sailors." When his message was leaked to the *San Francisco Chronicle*, the captain was removed from his post.

"We all have one mission and that's to defend the nation," said then Secretary of the Navy Thomas Modly, who removed Crozier, as he suggested the sailors at risk were dispensable. As of June 10, twelve hundred of the forty-eight-hundred crew members aboard the USS *Theodore Roosevelt* had contracted the coronavirus.

If soldiers and veterans are so disposable, what does matter to the deepest pocket of our tax dollars, the US Department of Defense?

Since the inception of the pandemic, the Washington consensus assured that major weapons makers such as Lockheed Martin and Raytheon would receive payment in advance of work. The chief pandemic profiteer, Lockheed Martin, received an estimated $450 million to keep its supply chain for weapons funded. So generous is the advance funding that the company was advertising thousands of new jobs while millions of unemployed waited desperately for their belated $1,200 aid and relief payments from the federal government.

Elsewhere, tucked away in the US House of Representatives Heroes Act was a provision to reimburse defense contractors not only for unemployed workers but also for executives' salaries and business costs of marketing and sales.

Why the preference for the industry of war and death over its vets and soldiers? For one, the Pentagon is driven to remain the macho military superpower of the world, given China's economic prowess. Marshall Billingslea, the US arms control negotiator, set his sights on spending Russia and China "into oblivion" in an arms race. Secretary of Defense Mark Esper worried that the three-trillion-dollar infusion into the economy for, among others, the sixteen percent unemployed by late June, 2020—those who can't pay for rent or food or medications—"may throw us off course of increasing the defense budget three to five percent."

Every "good" in our federal discretionary budget—education, housing, health, renewable energy, diplomacy, and more is cut in Trump's proposed 2021 budget while weapons of mass destruction, fossil fuels, anti-immigration staffing and resources are increased. Worse, the US DOD has insulated weapons manufacturers from the economic crash of COVID in order to assure our military dominance in the world.

With a new administration, we have a chance to cut the defense budget. However, as one analyst writes, "even the most liberal legislators are likely to rush to the defense of plants (and jobs) in their own district." But an aggressive Green New Deal here could replace lost defense jobs with solar and wind technology jobs.

We need to redefine our militarized national security embodied in weapons and global top cop mentality as urgently as cities and states need to rethink community security embodied in militarized police. We need to replace the *necessary* arms industry with a *more necessary* Green New Deal that can revive our economy, slow the climate crisis upon us, and forge a path to peace in our world.

Originally published June 29, 2020 in the *Daily Hampshire Gazette*. Reprinted with permission.

War and Militarism: Our Nemesis

The law of the gun has devastated the condition of women.

—Amy Smythe
UN representative to the Congo conflict

The sorrows of war have preoccupied and sometimes haunted me for decades going back to the American war in Vietnam when the evening news, for the first time, carried realistic war footage. All that I have learned since—from testimony; biography and autobiography of war victims and repentant veterans; realistic, non-embedded coverage of wars; and UN studies—is that non-combatants, non-aggressors, unarmed, internally displaced, and refugees are war's most dreadful and tragic victims, none more so than women and children.

It was a seminar on the public health effects of war in my department at Boston University School of Public Health that set the course of my life since retiring in 2009. I chose to speak in that seminar on the health effects of war on women, a topic that led me to much soul-troubling reading about rampant sexual violation of women during war, in refugee camps, and during post-war occupation. Being an environmental engineer led me to probe the effects of war on the environment—again facing another shock that the US Pentagon is the major institutional contributor to the climate crisis worldwide. Further, the Pentagon and its military contractors account for the largest number of extremely toxic US Environmental Protection Agency Superfund sites in the United States.

Joining the Traprock Center for Peace and Justice was my first political act once I returned fulltime to my home in western

Massachusetts. And thus began a journey of writing, speaking, protesting, initiating partnerships and collaborative projects, many here and others in Vietnam, Sierra Leone, and with Lebanese NGOs working with Syrian women war refugees, all with Traprock as a sheltering canopy.

Both war and militarism are portrayed in federal government press briefings and news clips as black and white realities: "good guys vs. bad guys" and "protecting the homeland from terrorists." In the past few years, China and Russia—each for different alleged security reasons—have risen, in the US State Department and Pentagon purview, to first place as enemy threats to US security and status in the world. A cold war among so-called Great Powers, already in the making, threatens to become a hot war, especially with China, while diplomatic intelligence and wisdom are in short supply. China, let us note, has one foreign military base in the East African country of Djibouti while the United States commands a global military empire with some eight hundred military bases in foreign countries across the world and overseas territories.

The writings I have chosen to include expose the manifold destructive consequences of industrial war on the environment, on solders and veterans, on civilians, on women and children, on the peoples we labeled the "bad guys," and on our federal budget, which privileges war and militarism above all of our human and social needs. Nor is US militarism a recent phenomenon since the post-World War II Cold War: the roots go deep, as revealed by book reviews included in the following.

Some ten years ago, in the conviction that there is no peace without justice, we added the word "justice" to Traprock's name. We include all facets of justice: justice for women, racial justice, economic justice, health justice, and environmental justice. Taxes are moral documents: if social and environmental justice urgencies underpinned our federal discretionary budget, we would necessarily shrink our war budget and invest in healthcare for all, housing as a human right, equal opportunity for education, and a living wage for all. With a robust Green New Deal, we could re-right our national and international priorities and forge *warheads into windmills*.

One Holy Night
co-written with Frances Crowe

Along the western front of World War I lie miles of cemeteries for British, Scottish, Belgian, French, and other soldiers killed in the war. In a lone, out-of-the way plot in that land of teenage war dead, a large cross and a dozen small ones honor the Christmas truce of 1914 spontaneously celebrated by soldiers and even some officers on both sides of the war. By five months into the merciless war, they were living in freezing trenches with corpses and rats that fed on the human dead, so-called warring sides facing each other through rows of barbed wire and exposed to artillery shells, machine guns, and, later, poison gas.

The tale of the 1914 Christmas truce survived through letters and photos of soldiers who, in many locations along six hundred miles of trenches in Belgium and France, suspended war and shared Christmas, like brothers, with their enemy. One story tells of a young German soldier singing "Stille Nacht," "Silent Night," on Christmas Eve and, from nearby trenches, other soldiers joining in their own tongues.

What followed was the most unique of nights in what we know of the history of war: soldiers on both sides laid down their weapons, crossed over barbed wire and shell holes, and greeted each other with Christmas gifts of food, beer, champagne, and schnapps. Together they buried corpses of the fallen that lay in the narrow no-man's land between them, played soccer with tin cans and straw-filled sandbags for balls, sang carols, took photos, and exchanged mementos and addresses.

Fraternizing like that is treasonous as it undermines war morale and the indoctrinated will to kill. And thus, military authorities anticipated and suppressed a Christmas truce with "the so-called enemy" the following year.

Erich Maria Remarque enlisted at nineteen in the World War I German army. Quickly he saw that a sense of the ideal and almost romance of war, instilled by the state's propaganda campaign, turned high school boys like him into willing recruits for slaughter. Some ten years after the war's end, he published his first, and what some consider the greatest, antiwar novel, *All Quiet on the Western Front*.

Remarque's nineteen-year-old soldier and central character acutely observes the corrupt dynamics of war:

> I see how peoples are set against each other . . . foolishly, innocently, obediently slaying each other . . . While they (careerist politicians and media war boosters) continue to talk and write, we saw the wounded and dying . . . The wrong people do the fighting.

In perhaps the most incisive moment of the novel, a young German soldier gazes upon a young French soldier he has killed and ponders their common humanity.

> Why do they never tell us that you are poor devils like us, that your mothers are just as anxious as ours, and that we have the same fear of death, and the same dying, and the same agony.

That war to end all wars did the opposite. It sowed the seeds of future wars. The model of industrial warfare—bombing cities, employing chemical poisons, and a punitive peace treaty with the winners dividing up the empires of the losers—all but guaranteed that future conflicts would be settled by military force, not skilled diplomacy and politics.

George Ball, a banker and diplomat who served as part of management in the state department under Presidents Kennedy and Johnson, observed that no one in those administrations was assigned to study a diplomatic solution to end the Vietnam War. In 1963 and again in 1967, President Charles de Gaulle of France offered to mediate a truce, but the United States was determined to win militarily lest a defeat or stalemate be perceived by the world as weakness and, thus, embolden Communism. Millions of Vietnamese and tens of thousands of Americans lost their lives senselessly for US image in the world, image ultimately tarnished by the extreme brutality of our war on a small, poor country of peasants.

The seeds of our military interventions into Iraq and Syria, with aerial bombing and at least some three thousand soldiers on the ground to defeat the lawless and sadistic Islamic State of Iraq and the Levant, ISIS, were sown during the second Iraq War. The eight-year war, built on a base of deceit and lies, left Iraq a failed state and a bitterly divided country where up to one million of twenty-four million people died, millions fled as war refugees, and women's equality was set back decades—a breeding ground, in other words, for terrorism.

The youthful soldiers' truce on Christmas 1914 was but a moment of sanity in the adult men's insane war fought for empire and reckless power alliances. May their inspired act be—more than a hundred years later—a beacon for diplomacy and political solutions. "For what can war but endless war still breed," in the words of British poet John Milton.

A galvanizing presence, the late antinuclear and antiwar activist Frances Crowe spoke truth to power for many decades as, from her Northampton base, she led others in honoring conscience.

Originally published December 17, 2014 in the *Greenfield Recorder*.

Forty-Two Years in Afghanistan:
Can a New US Foreign Policy Avoid Hyper-Masculinist Ego?

Every member of Congress attended the September 14, 2001, memorial service at the Washington National Cathedral for the nearly three thousand victims of September 11 attacks that year in New York City, Washington DC, and Pennsylvania. In that service, Reverend Nathan Baxter, dean of the cathedral, invoked "Let us also pray for divine wisdom as our leaders consider the necessary actions for national security . . . that as we act we not become the evil we deplore."

Representative Barbara Lee had "agonized over her vote" until the morning she listened to the prayer. That afternoon, the Senate voted 98 to 0 giving President Bush open-ended authorization for war. The House voted 420 to 1 for the same. Representative Lee was the sole exception as she restated Reverend Baxter's warning, "As we act, let us not become the evil we deplore."

Deadly Sins of the US War in Afghanistan

In 2021, Congress together with the US Executive Branch, Pentagon, and military contractors should return to the National Cathedral to confess their deadly sins of deceit, revenge, greed, and wrongful pride committed prior to and throughout the US war in Afghanistan. Is there penance enough for what the US government has wrought in extreme retaliation for 9/11? For example:

- seventy-one thousand Afghani and Pakistani civilian deaths from bombs, bullets, blasts, and fire, and
- more than two trillion US blood dollars wasted on that war of vengeance

Afghanistan is poorer, more corrupt, more misogynist than it was before we first intervened forty-two years ago.

Deceit

Beginning in 1979 and through the 1980s, the United States trained, armed, and funded Islamic jihadists, mujahedin, among them Osama Bin Laden. Mujahedin morphed into the Taliban and al-Qaeda. The US goal, expressed in 1979 by Secretary of State Zbigniew Brzezinski to President Carter, was to give "the USSR its Vietnam War." Why? Because the Soviet Union supported the then-socialist, secular government in Afghanistan, one that guaranteed rights for women and minorities.

Thus, we laid a foundation for 9/11, for our subsequent twenty-year war in Afghanistan, and for consequent, endless global war on terrorism. Afghan women and girls lost their gains in equality, education, and rights in 1992 when the US-backed mujahedin defeated the socialist government. Four years later, the Taliban defeated the mujahedin government. After the US vanquished the Taliban in December 2001, it installed its preferred Afghani leaders.

Featuring sensation over substance, the corporate media failed to give the public an informed understanding of the twenty-year war, its rudderless nature, and corruption of our contractors and our chosen Afghan political leaders, all documented by the US Inspector General for the war.

Revenge

Rather than a manhunt for bin Laden, which the Taliban government expressed willingness to cooperate with in 2001, and a legal trial in the United States if he were caught alive, our government chose to devastate Afghanistan, the then-second poorest country in the world, none of whose people had participated in 9/11.

Greed

Military weapons industries, their boards, bought politicians, and their investors— all merchants of death—and the Taliban are the sole winners of the twenty-year war. Outperforming the market by fifty-eight percent, ten thousand dollars invested in defense-contractor stocks on 2001 grew to nearly a hundred thousand dollars in 2021. The war was an endless money pit for US contractors and Afghan warlords, as testified to by US veterans.

Wrongful Pride/Vanity

US policymakers must act quickly to mitigate the damage to American's global credibility, according to the August 26, 2021 edition of Defense News. Lest Europe and Russia see the US as weak, the government must strengthen our military posture in the Baltic and Black Sea regions, Defense News advises. The US looks diminished to our likely next war priority—China. Initiate greater allied Asian naval exercises to project American strength and leadership, Defense News says. Biden must "lead from front."

Can the United States adopt a new foreign policy based not on militaristic, hyper-masculinist ego but on peace and problem solving? That's our real challenge.

Misogyny: Woman-Hating

The Taliban are among the most women-hating men in the world, and their interim government is vacant of women. We owe open-door priority to Afghan women seeking refuge in our country, and so also do the other thirty-eight countries engaged in the war. We need, writes Malala Yousafzai, nearly killed by the Taliban for pursuing her education, "specific agreements that girls can complete their education, can go to university, and be allowed to join the workforce with jobs they choose."

If our government's alleged goal is to "promote peace, modernity, and democratic values," then I say learn from women. We women have almost universally won our rights, tactically and intelligently across history, without using warplanes, drones, soldiers, bombs, or guns.

Originally published September 21, 2021 at juancole.com. Reprinted with permission.

War and Warming

Can We Save the Planet Without Taking on the Pentagon?

If we are not united in peace, we cannot save the planet.

—Thich Nhat Hanh

Looking out to my audience of young climate change activists and older peace activists gathered for a talk and discussion on "war and warming," I see in the generational difference what many peace activists perceive. Peace, war, militarism, and nuclear weapons are an agenda of another era—while progressive political energy today is galvanized by climate change. One climate activist explained that, in his lifetime, no nuclear weapons had been used while climate change had worsened. Thus, our movements largely work in silos despite the actuality that war and fossil fuels have been fatally codependent since World War II.

Oil is indispensable for war and militarism. Think of it as the lifeblood coursing through our foreign policy, a policy based on maintaining superpower status and confronting those whom we perceive as challenging us with force. The 1980 Carter Doctrine, which stated that the United States would use military force if necessary to defend its national interests in the Persian Gulf, formalized the toxic nexus between access to oil and war. Since the late 1970s, the United States has spent more than eight trillion dollars through ongoing naval patrols in an effort to protect oil cargoes in the Persian Gulf.

Keeping oil and gas supply sea lanes open in the South China Sea in the face of China's expansionism there is a factor in the US pivot to Asia. The foreign policy pivot has involved engaging Australia and Southeast Asian allies in military training exercises, opening new bases and those previously closed to the US military, and sales of new weapons systems. Further, the Obama administration prioritized a military so-called "triangular alliance" with Japan, pressuring the country to abandon its peace constitution, and South Korea, where the US has a military foothold on the Asian continent, for countering North Korea and the rising power of China. Such ratcheting up of military dominance is reliant on oil, the lifeline of weaponry, military exercises, and war.

War for oil has come home. Militarized North Dakota police attacked nonviolent water protectors protesting the Dakota Access oil pipeline with rubber bullets, tear gas, concussion grenades, and water cannons in sub-freezing temperatures. One medic treating injuries described it as a "low grade war."

A thumbnail sketch of recent US spending confirms the axiom that *war culture is a defining feature of US politics*. In 2016, as in previous years, an estimated one trillion dollars was allocated by Congress to military defense, militarized national security, veterans, and debt from recent wars. In that same year, a few billion dollars—crumbs from the master's table—were allocated to research and development for energy efficiency and renewable energy technologies. Between 2010-2015, the federal government invested fifty-six billion dollars in clean energy internationally, while it recently committed to one trillion dollars, closer as the twenty-first century advanced, to two trillion, for modernizing nuclear weapons, their infrastructure, and their delivery systems by 2030.

What's clear from US spending priorities is that access to oil, predatory capitalism, and military dominance has governed US policy in the world.

Militarism: an Engine of Climate Change

In 1940, the United States military consumed one percent of the country's total fossil fuel. By the end of World War II, the military's share rose to twenty-nine percent. Militarism is the most oil-intensive activity on the planet and grows more so with faster, bigger, more fuel-guzzling planes, tanks, and naval vessels. At the outset of the Iraq War in March 2003, the army estimated it would need more than forty million gallons of gasoline for three weeks of combat, thus exceeding the total quantity used by all Allied forces in the four years of World War 1.

The frequency and prevalence of US armed conflict since World War II is another factor in the combustible mix of war and warming. One count has documented 153 instances of US armed forces engaged in conflict abroad from 1945 through 2004, a number consistent with other estimates. That count, though, does not include covert military missions when US Special Operations Forces, larger in number than the active-duty militaries of many countries, operate in 135 countries. Nor do the 153 military conflicts since 1945 include US occupation forces stationed abroad since World War II, military participation in mutual security organizations such as the North Atlantic Treaty Organization or NATO, military base agreements for the estimated 750-1000 US military bases across the planet, and routine oil-intensive military training exercises around the globe.

After an unprecedented investigation into military use of fossil fuels, Barry Sanders, author of *The Green Zone* in 2009, calculated that the US military consumed as much as one million barrels of oil per day and contributed five percent of current global warming emissions, more than the majority of countries.

Climate Change in a Militarizing World

Climate change is inevitably an issue of peace because the Pentagon is the single largest institutional contributor of climate change emissions in the world. And as the Pentagon goes, so go the military budgets of other major powers. "We are not your enemy," a Chinese strategist told journalist John Pilger, " but if you (in the West) decide we are, we must prepare without delay."

According to some security analysts, talk of fighting terrorism fills the media but is secondary in the talk of US and NATO generals, admirals, and defense ministers. Many politicians in western nations and NATO believe that war between NATO countries or the United States and the great powers of Russia and/or China is not only possible but may break out at any time. Therefore, bigger spending in all involved countries on high-tech weapons, deploying more forces, and more military joint exercises will exacerbate climate change emissions and heighten the potential for nuclear war, thus risking another kind of climate change—nuclear winter.

Growing global militarization portends greater military buildup in Russia, China, NATO, and the Middle East and greater climate change emissions. The United States expends thirty-seven percent of the global military budget, and its military is estimated to contribute five percent of climate change emissions. Can we not, then, assume that the rest of the world's military spending, weapons manufacturing, military exercises, and conflict combine to bring military related fossil fuel emissions to near fifteen percent of global climate change pollution? Intensifying military tensions will drive that pollution higher and could vitiate country commitments to the Paris climate agreement.

War mirrors the culture of a country. US militarism—from its training, tactics, and logistics to its reasons for going to war and its weapons of war—is distinctly shaped by core elements of American identity. Determining cultural forces are, according to military historian Victor Hansen, manifest destiny, frontier mentality, rugged individualism, unfettered market capitalism, and what he calls a "muscular independence," force projection in Pentagon-speak. The eminently masculinist qualities converge to generate bigger, better, and more destructive war technology. And they delivered up a bullying, white nationalist, law-breaking billionaire and sexual predator as president in 2016.

The US habit and competence for war, with its origins in the near annihilation of Native Americans, may be our society's nemesis unless we do critical soul-searching about our cultural and personal values and actively engage in transforming them. Let us remember and honor the plentitude of activist, nonviolent movements in our society that have profoundly challenged the dominant patriarchal profile of our culture described by Hanson. Among them are:

- the movement to end violence against women and achieve equal rights for women
- the civil, immigrant, and indigenous rights movements
- the antiwar and peace movements
- the Black Lives Matter movement
- Standing Rock water protectors
- progressive media
- peace and justice studies
- progressive labor and health workers
- the coop, sustainable agriculture, and Transition Town movements
- pervasive radical activism to stop climate change, and
- victories against fracking and oil pipelines

The challenge is how to build voice, social cohesion, and public influence for our shared values of a sense of human community, our core connection as humans with nature, our empathy with the exploited, and our thirst for equality and justice for all.

In times of overt authoritarian and corporate control, our hope for turning the tide will come from local, community-based campaigns and actions, including:

- anti-fracking ordinances, town by town
- the fight for fifteen-dollar minimum wage city by city
- churches and cities providing sanctuary for undocumented workers
- redefining and reconstituting community security
- children suing their government for their right to clean energy and a livable future
- campaigns against all forms of violence against girls and women
- using community media to promote equal rights for all, and
- electing people to local and regional office who champion those issues and campaigns

Working together, we must turn the tide on those destructive forces and seek enduring peace _on_ earth and enduring peace _with_ earth.

Originally presented as a talk given to a joint 350.orgCT and Promoting Enduring Peace Center, New Haven, forum in 2016.

Originally published January 28, 2017, at *Portside*. Reprinted with permission.

Setting the Course of US Wars, Military Expansion, and Overthrow of Governments

The True Flag: Theodore Roosevelt, Mark Twain, and the Birth of American Empire
by Stephen Kinzer
St. Martin's Griffin. 2017

By the final decade of the nineteenth century, the American project sanctified as Manifest Destiny was complete. The western boundary of the United States stretched to the Pacific Ocean, leaving in its wake the genocide of Native Americans, the purchase of Louisiana without *the consent of the governed*, and a war of aggression against Mexico. What next? Pursue the colonialist mandate beyond continental borders—or not?

Stephen Kinzer's *The True Flag: Theodore Roosevelt, Mark Twain, and the Birth of the Empire* is a compact, bracing history of the answer to *What next?* It features the drama and decisions of four years–1898-1902–that, in Kinzer's thesis, set the course of American wars, military expansion, and overthrow of governments throughout the twentieth and into the twenty-first century, interrupted with brief, impermanent periods of so-called isolationism.

The author collates the eloquent rhetoric and caustic debates between expansionist members of Congress, including alpha male Theodore Roosevelt, aristocrat Henry Cabot Lodge, media giant William Randolph Hearst, and prominent anti-empire social critics and populist orators including Mark Twain, William Jennings Bryan, and steel magnate and philanthropist Andrew Carnegie to capture vividly the divided political passions and high stakes of the day.

The empire builders used robust, positively coded terms like "the large policy" to label their aspirations for America's preeminence among world powers and for the aggressive market ambitions of America's capitalists. The anti-imperialists warned of erosion of democracy at home, rise of plutocracy, and blowback from military subordination of other peoples against their will and forecasted what, a century later, Chalmers Johnson incisively named the "sorrows of empire."

The Spanish-American War of 1898 was the spark that inflamed the US quest for overseas colonies. It began with Cuba and quickly stolen Puerto Rico, then the Philippines, Guam seized en route to the Philippines, and Hawaii–all in nine months. In public, expansionists framed the takeovers as beneficent, rescuing oppressed and backwards people to catechize and civilize them.

Independence movements in Cuba, the Philippines, and Hawaii were brutally suppressed. Hundreds of thousands of people were killed, particularly in the Philippines, which waged guerrilla warfare until defeated in 1902. While American soldiers tortured and assassinated prisoners, burned villages, and killed farm animals in a precursor to the later American war in Vietnam, a pliant press followed military orders and carried no unfavorable coverage of the resistance.

The war in the Philippines was intensely terrorizing for women in particular. *The Anti-Imperialist* journal reported "American soldiers had turned Manila into a world center of prostitution."

Amplifying that too brief reference to the extreme toll of US militarism on women, Janice Raymond writes in *Not a Choice, Not a Job* that "US prostitution colonialism, especially during the Philippine-American War, created the model for the US military–prostitution complex in all parts of the world."

The system "assured US soldiers certified sexual access to Filipinas and became an intrinsic part of colonial practice in Cuba and Puerto Rico."

Meanwhile, the empire seekers rubbed their covetous hands over the prospect of new customers for manufactured goods and, in the case of the Philippines, a springboard to Chinese and Japanese markets. Military bases in the Philippines and Guam would follow to protect and project US economic and military power in East Asia.

Kinzer's considerable talent joins meticulous research and engaging stories with a canine ability to sniff out the lies beneath the platitudes that sold the public on war. What he foregrounds so credibly are the oversized male egos of "large policy" politicians with more morally grounded and prescient anti-imperialist crusaders. Among them are Booker T. Washington who, in speaking against US imperialism abroad, warned that the cancer in our midst—racism, the legacy of slavery—will prove to be as dangerous to the country's well-being as an attack from without. Many African American anti-imperialist groups emerged and assailed US imperialism for its intrinsic white racist arrogance.

With much detail and nuance, Kinzer tracks the fatal flaws of the immensely talented and populist orator William Jennings Bryan who, for his contrarian vote that sealed the doom of the Philippines, helped determine the fate of our country's future as an empire. Likewise, the seemingly passive aggressive William McKinley, elected in 1896 and again in 1900, is unmasked as the imperialist he grew to be over the course of his presidency.

The final chapter, "The Deep Hurt," traces the arc of US militarism across the twentieth century and into the twenty-first—a long and unfinished arc that is neither moral nor does it bend toward justice. At each end of that ongoing arc, the words of two military veterans of US foreign wars distill and corroborate Kinzer's stateside exposé in *The True Flag*. Brigadier General Smedley Butler, born in 1881, began his career as a teenage Marine combat soldier assigned to Cuba and Puerto Rico during the US invasion of those islands. He fought next in the US war in the Philippines, ostensibly against Spanish imperialism but ultimately against the Philippine revolution for independence. Next he was assigned to fight against China during the Boxer Rebellion and was also stationed in Guam. He gained the highest rank and a host of medals during subsequent US occupations and military interventions in Central America and the Caribbean, popularly known as the Banana Wars.

As Butler confessed in his iconoclastic book, *War Is a Racket*, he was "a bully boy for American corporations," making countries safe for US capitalism. More isolationist than antiwar, he nonetheless nailed the war profiteers—racketeers in his unsparing lexicon—for the blood on their hands as bracingly as any pacifist. War is the oldest, most profitable racket, he writes—one in which billions of dollars are made for millions of lives destroyed.

Making the world "safe for democracy" was, at its core, making the world safe for war profits. Of diplomacy Butler wrote, "The state department is always talking about peace but thinking about war." He proposed an "Amendment for Peace" that meant in essence, keep the military—the army, navy, and marines in the days before the air force—in the continental US for purposes of defense against military invasions here.

And in the twenty-first century, Major Danny Sjursen, who served tours with reconnaissance units in Iraq and Afghanistan, proposes that the US Department of Defense should be renamed the US Department of Offense. His reasons:

+ American troops are deployed in seventy percent of the world's countries
+ American pilots were bombing seven countries as he wrote, and
+ the US, alone among nations, has divided the six human inhabited continents into six military commands

Our military operations exceed US national interests and are "unmoored" from reasoned strategy and our society's needs, Major Sjursen concludes.

For all of the strengths of *The True Flag*, one glaring lacuna is the minimalist presence of women in Kinzer's depiction of the early anti-imperialist movement. *The True Flag* is premised on history as made by "great men" good and bad. A "great woman" of the era, Jane Addams, elected vice-president of the Anti-Imperialist League after a brilliant speech, has only a bit part. Addams was renowned not only for her settlement house work at Hull House in Chicago but also for speaking out unceasingly against imperialism and war. The FBI kept a file on her, and she was labeled among the most dangerous women in America. The author overlooked her influence in the era.

A second lacuna is omitting the original sins of imperial America—the genocide of Native Americans for their land and the enslavement of Africans, which ultimately became the combustion engine of US capitalism. Ironically, it was the pro empire exhorters of 1898 who used the exploitative expansion within the early US to defend extending Manifest Destiny to the Pacific region. The Lebanese poet Khalil Gibran could have penned his words from 1933 for our national dilemma today:

> Pity the nation that acclaims the bully as hero and that deems the glittering conqueror bountiful . . .

Originally published October 27, 2017 at *Truthdig*. Reprinted with permission.

Ongoing Structural Impacts of World War II
The Violent American Century: War and Terror Since World War II
by John Dower
Haymarket Books. 2017

In 1941, Henry Luce, the mogul of influential and popular magazines from *Time* and *Life* to *Fortune* and *Sports Illustrated*, declared the twentieth century the American Century. By the gauge of prosperity, power, and influence, the United States emerged from World War II as the defining leader of the so-called "Free World," and with the dissolution of the Soviet Union in 1991, of the entire world.

The historian John Dower borrows Luce's "American Century" as a heuristic device in tracing the lengthening arc of US dominance in weapon development, militarism, and military empire—without peer in history—since World War II. Thus, his title *The Violent American Century: War and Terror Since World War II*.

With exceptional concision, Dower delineates the ongoing structural impacts of World War II to frame more thoroughly and intricately than do US textbooks and war hagiography the war's influence on most subsequent conflicts and world politics. Dower writes that the "good war," as it has been christened and cleansed, was "the apogee of industrialized total war." Civilians in cities were targets of strategic bombing by the US and Britain. New weapons of mass destruction, atomic bombs, were developed and used. Countries including Korea, Vietnam, Germany, and China were left "explosively divided."

Among the war's legacies are, according to Dower:

+ global financial and political institutions, the most idealistic being the United Nations with its Universal Declaration of Human Rights
+ pathbreaking war crimes trials though the victors never tried themselves for war crimes, and
+ the eventual end of European colonialism

On the bleaker side, World War II concluded with a hostile, divided world and a burgeoning military/Congressional/industrial complex that has governed US response to conflict ever since.

The Cold War with its nuclear terror and proxy wars in Korea and Southeast Asia, the US transition to sole superpower status in the 1990s, according to Dower, and post-9/11 wars—all are examined with a lens that captures what Dower calls the "essentially bipolar" nature of American macro behavior in the world. Dower describes it as "hubristic and overwhelmingly powerful by material measures, yet fearful and insecure." Think, says Dower, compulsive national anxiety over an alleged missile gap with the Soviets in the fifties and early sixties, the domino theory of the sixties and seventies positing that one country's becoming communist would cause surrounding countries to do so also, the obsession with getting over failure in Vietnam in the seventies and eighties, and the manic fear of terrorism today. Fear of menacing "existential enemies primed the political pump to maintain support for a massive military machine" and the expansion of a national security state, according to Dower.

A balance of terror via nuclear weapons buildup marked forty years of US-Soviet bombast and confrontation. US military planners projected nuclear bomb attacks on the Soviet Union and China that would kill hundreds of millions of Russians and Chinese. Only recently have once-prominent insiders, including General George Lee Butler, commander of the Strategic Air Command in the early 1990s, and William Perry, secretary of defense in the Clinton administration, passionately critiqued that psychopathology of deterrence.

A provocative current runs through the book, one that challenges current dogma on the decline in global violence and inclination toward global peace since 1945. The proposition of a more peaceful world is based in good part on fewer conflict-related deaths since World War II and the trend in precision weapons. Dower counters that conclusion with a multitude of examples, including the growing conflict-based refugee crisis that approaches that of World War II, "the political harm to democracy" from the colossal post-9/11 national security state devoted to sustaining "a state of semi-war," and the costs of war that magnify our debt for decades to come.

Dower opens and closes his book with the acknowledgement that America's "prosperity and professed ideals are still beacons to many," reinforcing the mystique of exceptionalism despite the government's "intoxication with brute force."

How does the top global military superpower and largest trader in weapons of war remain a beacon of democratic ideals?

A Nigerian friend living in Europe recently provided a partial response. She noted that pervasive counter demonstrations and persistent citizen protest against the Trump administration's policies—protests against banning Muslims and on behalf of women's rights, Black lives, and climate science—reflect our country's ideals of freedom of expression, equality, and tolerance to the world.

Side by side with widespread democratic resistance to domestic policies, there is, however, a national quietism about the seemingly unstoppable full spectrum, international dominance envisioned by both political parties since World War II, as distilled in *The Violent American Century*. Administrations from both parties, for example, engaged directly and indirectly in the overthrow of at least two-dozen Latin American governments between 1948 and

1990. Central Intelligence Agency, CIA, manuals on torture and the US Army's School of the Americas, popularly dubbed School of Assassins, have trained right-wing Latin American military officers and police in tactics to conduct the "dirty wars" that ravaged so many South American countries.

Hundreds of billions spent since 9/11 on foreign military training in more than 150 countries and combating terrorism globally have resulted in increasing the likelihood of military-backed coups by those trained, with no evidence of promoting democracy. Yet too few—in media and the American public—are aware of or troubled by that underbelly of US exceptionalism.

Trump's simplistic encomium for the US military was consonant with former President Barack Obama's staccato declaration in his 2016 State of the Union address:

> The United States of America is the most powerful nation on earth. Period. Period. It's not even close. It's not even close. It's not even close. We spend more on our military that the next eight nations combined.

President Biden continues in this tradition of US military triumphalism.

Seventy-six years of American Century have brought us to this: our standout claim to fame is military muscularity (and record wealth), while our status among all democratic nations on health, education, prisons, commitment to the global climate accord, and economic, gender, and racial equality has only declined.

> *A nation that continues year after year to spend*
> *more money on military defense than on programs of*
> *social uplift is approaching spiritual doom.*
> —Martin Luther King Jr.

Originally published June 20, 2018 at *Truthdig*. Reprinted with permission.

Two Roads Diverged
co-written with Frances Crowe

On June 10, 1963, President John F. Kennedy delivered a commencement address at American University that, in fewer than thirty minutes, turned traditional national security policy on its head. Kennedy proclaimed that world peace is "the most important topic on earth—not merely peace for Americans but peace for all men and women—not merely peace in our time but peace for all time."

His speech was hailed by then Soviet Union Premier Nikita Khrushchev as "the greatest speech by any American President since Roosevelt."

Eight months earlier, both men had faced the terrifying possibility of nuclear holocaust in a showdown between the United States and the Soviet Union, remembered to history as the Cuban Missile Crisis. Shaken but emboldened by it, Kennedy laid out a principled, strategic, and humanistic vision for ending the arms race and dissipating the hostile Cold War rhetoric and culture. He led by example in honoring the Russian people "for their many achievements—in science and space, in economic and industrial growth, in culture and in acts of courage," alluding to twenty million Russians killed in World War II. And he announced a proposed direct line of communication between Moscow and Washington.

Within two months of his commencement address, both former Cold War antagonists and Britain signed the Partial Nuclear Test Ban Treaty, prohibiting nuclear testing in the atmosphere, outer space, and under water, resulting in substantial reduction of radioactive contamination. President Kennedy was assassinated before being able to construct a path toward complete and permanent disarmament.

Let us contrast Kennedy's words and convictions expressed on June 10, 1963, with our government's twenty-first century national defense posture. Those two diverging roads—Kennedy's, the one less traveled by, and present century's—lie before us.

JFK

What kind of peace do we seek? Not one enforced on the world by American weapons of war. I am talking about the kind of peace that enables people to hope and to build a better life for their children—not merely peace for Americans but peace for all men and women.

Stockpiling weapons—nuclear and non-nuclear—"is not the only" nor the most efficient means of achieving peace, he continues. Both the United States and the Soviet Union are devoting massive sums of money that could be better devoted to combatting ignorance, poverty, and disease. New weapons beget new counter weapons.

The Pentagon:

2018 opened with a new National Defense Posture embracing the concept that the greatest threat to US national security and prosperity is now Russia and China with terrorism relegated to a second tier. Elsewhere, the Pentagon spoke of four-plus-one threats: Russia, China, North Korea, Iran, and terrorism. The military's chief concern was that the 2018-2019 defense budget—morbidly obese by comparison with the funds dedicated to diplomacy—was not large enough for conducting war on all those fronts.

President Donald J. Trump's national defense budget for the next fiscal year, passed overwhelmingly by House Republicans and Democrats, allocated eighteen times more funding—$717 billion—to military defense than to his proposed budget for diplomacy—$39 billion.

China's response to US war talk? The US has unparalleled military might as it spends three times more on military than China, remarked Chinese foreign ministry spokesman Geng Shuang. Yet its sense of insecurity is "beyond comprehension." He urged the US to abandon its confrontation mindset and move with the trend of the times, toward multipolarity, that is, numerous power centers in the world. Bluntly put: get used to sharing power with other regions, alliances, and countries.

JFK

The pursuit of peace is not as dramatic as the pursuit of war but we have no more urgent task. Too many of us think it is impossible. But that is a dangerous, defeatist belief. Our problems are man-made—therefore, they can be solved by us.

Resolving to end war for good is not a perfect guarantee, he continues, but it does offer "far more security and far fewer risks than an unabated, uncontrolled, unpredictable arms race."

"We can seek a relaxation of tensions without relaxing our guard," he says. What will that require, he asks. "Increased understanding" with our enemies, which requires "increased contact and communication." The goal is complete disarmament achieved in stages while building "new institutions of peace which would take the place of arms."

The Pentagon:

Since 9/11, we have expended more than $250 billion on training soldiers and security officers from at least 150 countries in the name of combatting terrorism and promoting democracy, international peace, and security. The results: no tangible national security benefit in the Middle East and African countries and no evidence of an increase in democratic values and civilian control of armed forces. If anything, the opposite—an increase of military-backed coups in the home countries of militaries we have trained. The program, according to a former US commanding officer for Africa, Carter Ham, succeeded in transmission of military skills, but failed to spend enough time on promoting good governance and democratic values.

Decades of Costly Wars

Andrew Bacevich, Vietnam veteran and foreign policy historian, asserts that the goal of the United States since the fall of the Soviet Union and end of the Cold War has been to remake the world in its own image, to "align everybody from A to Z—Afghanistan to Zimbabwe—with American values and the American way of life." With that goal, the US has embroiled itself for decades now in "a series of costly, senseless, unsuccessful, and ultimately counterproductive wars." Millions have been killed, countries broken, trillions in US war debt accumulated, and terrorism abroad and at home fueled.

JFK

If we cannot end now our differences, at least we can focus on our "common interests" and work to "make the world safe for diversity" of ideas, beliefs, forms of economy, and government. "For in the final analysis, we all inhabit this small planet. We all breathe the same air. We all cherish our children's future. And we are all mortal."

How far we have diverged as a country from that principled, strategic, and humanistic vision for our national security toward one of moral collapse. The road taken by Trump and his administration—clutching to military superpower status, abandoning the multiparty nuclear accord with Iran and the Paris climate agreement, threatening to use nuclear weapons, and eroding decades of environmental protection—leads only to hate, hostility, and extreme peril.

A galvanizing presence, the late antinuclear and antiwar activist Frances Crowe spoke truth to power for many decades as, from her Northampton base, she led others in honoring conscience.

Originally published June 8, 2018 in the *Berkshire Eagle*. Reprinted with permission.

Nuclear Weapons: 100 Seconds to Midnight

Western Massachusetts has a long and honorable history of mobilizing against nuclear weapons. Ending nuclear war and fostering non-violence were the animating mission of the Traprock Peace Center on Woolman Hill in Deerfield, Massachusetts in 1979. Randy Kehler, the first Traprock director, engaged hundreds of community members in launching, with other peace groups across the country, the Nuclear Weapons Freeze Campaign.

This national campaign, together with international sister campaigns, is credited with creating the political will for the Reagan/Gorbachev agreement in the late 1980s to eliminate short-range nuclear weapons and their launchers. Continuing in this political spirit, the Bush/Gorbachev agreement ultimately led to dismantling tens of thousands of nuclear weapons by Russia and the United States at the end of the Cold War.

More recently, two Northampton, Massachusetts-based organizing campaigns, Nuclearban.us and Back from the Brink work locally and nationally toward the goal of the US eliminating nuclear weapons and joining the landmark 2017 United Nations Treaty on the Prohibition of Nuclear Weapons, now international law.

The Traprock Center for Peace and Justice, in solidarity with thousands of peace organizations across the world, holds an annual vigil to commemorate the US dropping of atomic bombs on civilians in Hiroshima and Nagasaki, an act of human obliteration within a matter of seconds, never repeated by another country.

In our writings and interviews for local and national media in 2020, Traprock intentionally addressed the racism inherent in dropping the bombs on Japan. Some strong disagreement followed, and I responded with a letter to the editor. The articles that follow, published during 2020 and 2021, trace the advance made by atomic bomb survivors' or Hibakushas' unrelenting work until their deaths and that of hundreds of activist organizations against nuclear weapons. Their decades of activism catalyzed discussion and forums among UN non-nuclear countries in recent years, culminating in a 2017 UN vote that has resulted in an international law prohibiting any involvement with nuclear weapons for nations that have ratified the Treaty.

Nuclear nations may be the last to embrace and ratify this law. However, as banks, pension funds, and others continue to divest from nuclear weapons companies, those weapons will lose their legitimacy and the will for those weapons will erode. Moreover, we have precedents: the United States did sign the Chemical Weapons Convention and the Biological Weapons Convention.

As we enter 2021, the US is in a "full-blown arms race"–both nuclear and conventional–with Russia and China; and Iran and North Korea are building nuclear programs out of self-protection from US threats. Further, Trump had withdrawn from nuclear treaties and the 2017 nuclear accord with Iran; Saudi Arabia may have nuclear ambitions. Increasingly our department of defense, or more accurately, department of war, is flying nuclear-capable bombers ever closer to Russian and Chinese territory, stimulating a higher-paced arms race.

The Biden/Harris administration commences without our government having a coherent foreign policy on nuclear weapons, though President Biden has agreed upon a new five-year extension on the New START treaty with Russia. The treaty limits each country to a maximum of 1,550 deployed nuclear weapons. Aptly named, it is a *mere start*–hopefully and necessarily–to a nuclear weapons-free world.

On January 22, 2021, as the new UN law prohibiting any nuclear weapons involvement in countries that ratified the 2017 Treaty came into effect, William Perry, secretary of defense in the Clinton administration, traced the fourteen-year old high-level bipartisan consensus to abolish nuclear weapons. He cited Ronald Reagan's damning pronouncement: nuclear weapons are "totally irrational, totally inhumane, good for nothing but killing, possibly destructive of life and Earth and civilization." Perry wrote of the "power of the ought," describing our country's history of moving from "is" to "ought" in abolishing slavery and enfranchising women (though we have an arduous journey to eliminate racism and sexual violence). The nuclear weapons ban treaty, he concluded, "formally enshrines the necessity of their total elimination for the good of humanity."

On January 27, 2021 the Bulletin of the Atomic Scientists held the Doomsday Clock, a measure of the world's vulnerability to catastrophe, at a hundred seconds to midnight for the second consecutive year—the closest ever since its inception in 1947. There is no more urgent issue for the Biden administration than to restore a strong and decisive diplomatic approach to nuclear weapons with the goal of abolition of those demons. The majority of the world's citizens will it.

President Biden's budget for 2022 included funding for updating the country's nuclear weapons and delivery systems, thus showing no change in US policy about nuclear weapons of mass destruction.

Poets, Military Realists, and Millennials:
August 6 and 9

Give back my Father.
Give back my Mother.
Give Grandpa,
Grandma back;
Give my sons
and daughters back.
Give me back myself.

Give back
the human race.
As long as this life lasts,
this life,
Give back Peace
Peace that will never end.
—Sankichi Toge

At twenty-eight, Sankichi Toge suffered the atomic bombing at home, 1.8 miles from the epicenter in Hiroshima. After working tirelessly as an anti-war activist, he died at the National Hiroshima Sanatorium at the age of thirty-six. The poem "August 6 and 9" is engraved on his monument at the Hiroshima Peace Memorial Park.

Poet and writer, Kyoko Hayashi nearly died on August 9, 1945 in the atomic bombing of Nagasaki. She was fourteen years old and working at a factory less than a mile from the epicenter of the atomic explosion. She traveled barefoot for nine hours through the ruins of Nagasaki passing many dead and dying who had been crushed, burned, and mutilated beyond recognition.

The unique tragedy of those who lost their lives to the bomb, Hayashi feels, is that the bomb not only deprived them of their lives but also of "their own personal deaths." And for the survivors like herself, "the shortening of a given life, not being able to live fully—this was the promise made between an atomic bomb and its victims." The bomb changed time for her. "I could not make an appointment longer than a month ahead," given many hibakusha friends died from unpredictable bleeding. "The past is always present and the future is never countable."

In one of her many published stories, Hayashi invents a new calendar, the "A-bomb calendar" which designates 1945 as the first year. Why? "The significance of the birth of Christ or Buddha pales in comparison," with the event that demonstrated that "humans had gained the means to destroy their own species, all other species and the earth."

Fifty-four years after surviving the bomb, she journeyed from Japan to the Trinity Site in New Mexico, site of the first atomic bomb explosion, a national landmark since 1975, and "a hibakusha's birth place," as she deems it. She may be the sole atomic bomb survivor to have made this morbid pilgrimage.

Standing in Ground Zero at Trinity Site, she looks out to the red mountains and wilderness beyond and suddenly senses a kinship with desert plants and animals. "Until now as I stand at Trinity Site, I have thought it was we humans who were the first atomic bomb victims on Earth. I was wrong. Here are my senior hibakusha. They are here but cannot cry or yell."

Military Realists

Opposition to nuclear weapons has been unfailingly bipartisan since 1945. Key World War II military leaders from all branches of the armed forces, including generals Eisenhower, Arnold, Marshall, and MacArthur; and admirals Leahy, Nimitz, and Halsey strongly dissented, for both military and moral reasons, from President Harry Truman's decision to drop the bombs on two civilian Japanese cities, Hiroshima and Nagasaki. At their fortieth anniversary reunion in Los Alamos, New Mexico, seventy of 110 physicists who had worked on the atomic bomb signed a statement supporting nuclear disarmament.

No high-level military insider has renounced nuclear weapons so starkly and definitively as retired Air Force General Lee Butler, former commander of the Strategic Air Command that oversaw the entire nuclear arsenal. In December 1996, he used a National Press Club luncheon as his forum to urge his government to take the lead in abolishing all nuclear weapons. "Nuclear war," he said, "is a raging, insatiable beast whose instincts and appetites we pretend to understand but cannot possibly control." Nothing, he concluded, not peace through deterrence, nor national security, justifies those weapons of physical and genetic terror.

The pity here is that he waited until retirement to speak out.

One shaft of light—in this time of US complacence regarding our nearly two-trillion-dollar nuclear weapons so-called modernization program—are young people. In 2019 the International Committee of the Red Cross polled sixteen thousand millennials, ages twenty to thirty-five, from every region of the world regarding the use of nuclear weapons. Overall, a great majority, average eighty-four percent, responded that the use of nuclear weapons is "never acceptable," with strong agreement from those in nuclear-armed countries.

May the hibakusha and this generation guide us to global abolition of nuclear weapons.

Originally published August 4, 2020 in the *Greenfield Recorder*. Reprinted with permission.

Racism and the Atomic Bomb

When I stated in a recent *Recorder* article that dropping the atomic bombs on Hiroshima and Nagasaki was a racist act against non-white people, described as "vermin" and "rodents" that should be exterminated, Kathe Geist described the history underlying my statement as "sketchy." The atomic bomb was intended for use on Germany, she states in her letter to the *Recorder*, but Germany surrendered before the bomb was ready.

However, there is critical historical evidence underlying my statement. According to historian Richard Rhodes, author of Pulitzer Prize-winning *The Making of the Atomic Bomb*, President Franklin D. Roosevelt and Prime Minister Winston Churchill met in September, 1944, while we were still at war with Germany and Japan. In that meeting, they considered the bomb's first use should be on Japanese cities. The significance of that recorded meeting is that it contradicts the common historical opinion that Germany would have been bombed first if the atomic bomb had been ready to use before that country surrendered in June 1945.

There are further amplifying examples of the racist and spurious attitude that Japanese were subhuman and expendable, which would make using the atomic bomb on them more acceptable. Among them are the internment camps, where more than 110,000 Japanese Americans were imprisoned from 1942-1945. Yet, other "enemy" citizens, including Germans and Italians who happened to be white, were not. Polls at the time indicated that the majority of Americans approved.

Originally published September 2, 2020, as a letter to the editor in the *Greenfield Recorder*. Reprinted with permission.

Abolishing Nuclear Weapons: A New Chance

A nuclear darkness has engulfed the world for seven decades, with only intermittent breakthroughs of light when treaties among nuclear nations were negotiated. Some treaties have been violated for decades; others, walked away from by Trump. Any progress made on eliminating nuclear weapons has ceased. Worse, a new weapons upgrade is in the works by the nuclear nations. In 2009 President Obama spoke of the dream of a world without nuclear weapons, yet a handful of years later he put the US on course to spend nearly two trillion dollars on upgrading its nuclear weapons arsenal and delivery systems over a period of 30 years. Trump augmented the budget for the upgrade and added new nuclear weapons with threats to use them.

The seventy-year nuclear gloom began to lift on January 22, 2021. The nine countries that have held the world captive to the threat of nuclear war are losing moral ground to 122 smaller countries that approved the world's first nuclear weapons ban in July 2017. Once fifty of those 122 approving countries completed the ratification process of the UN Treaty for the Prohibition of Nuclear Weapons in their legislatures, it became international law in October 2020.

The law went into effect January 22, 2021 to the profound relief of most people of the world. Those now fifty-two *"freedom fighter"* countries commit to having nothing to do with nuclear weapons—no design, testing, manufacturing, financing, storage, transport, use or threat of use. Consider this a marathon for disarmament to outpace the current nuclear arms race in which all nuclear-armed countries are, in lockstep, upgrading their weapons.

And this is only the beginning. Thirty-five additional countries are in the process of ratifying the Treaty; fifty more support the Treaty; a dozen more have immense popular support, among them Canada, and are one election away from signing the Treaty. If the United States, where a majority of citizens does not want to use nuclear weapons, signed the Treaty, the rest would follow.

Actions of note:

+ the General Electric Company stopped production of nuclear weapons in 1993
+ two of the world's largest pension funds have divested from nuclear weapons
+ Mitsubishi UFG Financial Group, one of the five largest banks in the world, has excluded nuclear weapons production from its portfolio, labeling them "inhumane"
+ US President John F. Kennedy and Soviet Premier Nikita Khrushchev were working toward the abolition of nuclear weapons when Kennedy was assassinated, and
+ US President Ronald Reagan and Soviet Premier Mikhail Gorbachev agreed to a radical dismantling of their nuclear weapons

Our goal must be a world "without nuclear weapons . . . Nuclear war cannot be won and must never be fought," editorialized former Republican Secretary of State George Schultz and former Democrat Secretary of Defense William Perry.

Mayors for Peace: 7,675 cities in 163 countries support the total abolition of nuclear weapons.

Fifty-six former presidents, prime ministers, foreign and defense ministers from twenty NATO countries and Japan and South Korea recently signed an open letter in support of the UN treaty to ban nuclear weapons. "Sooner or later our luck will run out – unless we act. There is no cure for a nuclear war," they asserted. "Prevention is our only option."

Pope Francis: "The use of atomic energy for purposes of war is immoral as is the possession of atomic weapons."

A limited nuclear war could trigger a global famine that would likely end billions of lives. A full scale nuclear war would end human and most other life on Earth, reminding us of the classical depiction of total war: *they had to destroy the village to save it*. A nuclear war, whether by accident, misjudgment or intention to destroy the enemy would destroy the rest of us as well—how insane is that?

Sally Alley Muffin Stuffin of Wendell created a
Weapons into Windmills banner.
photo copyright by Anna György

What then can President Biden do?

- *Open dialogue* with and renew nuclear agreements and diplomacy with Russia immediately
- *Change US policy in three key ways*: no first use of nuclear weapons; take weapons off of hair trigger alert; and select another senior official to share decision–making about "pressing the button"
- *Revive the agreement with Iran*: they do not develop nuclear weapons; we lift sanctions
- With South Korea, *engage in diplomacy* with North Korea to freeze and roll back their nuclear weapons program
- *Stop* the new US program of upgrading nuclear weapons, and
- *Listen* to the world's majority and *lead* the United States toward signing the new UN Treaty, and the others will follow. It is our only solution to exit a dead-end system that permits a single human being, in the words of national security analyst Joseph Cirincione, "*to destroy in minutes all that humanity has constructed over millennia*"

Originally published January 22, 2021 in *the Greenfield Recorder*. Reprinted with permission.

Veterans: Living the Sorrows of War

A veteran told me a story, shared below, about the trauma of war to himself and his subsequent path to healing. Listening to veterans' bitter realism about war, reading their memoirs, and poring over studies from interviews with them has given me some of the deepest and most lucid reasons for working against war, militarism, and the gargantuan defense budget that funds both. Their face-to-face experience with the sorrows of war blows the cover off common justifications for incessant US militarism as fed to the American public in glib press conferences and nationalistic news, namely, claims of American exceptionalism with God on our side, national security premised on global military dominance, and peace through the sword.

How is it, though, that the US government can hail the military as keeper of world peace, as America's most patriotic institution, as comprised of America's most self-sacrificing citizens and then abandon so many veterans rendered homeless, suicidal, unable to work, and sick from war-related environmental exposures, as the following articles expose and explore?

Two writings on World War I and the Iraq War are reprinted from a series published by *Truthout, Listening to Soldiers and Vets. Truthout* says,

> The series features the voices of soldiers and veterans from armed conflicts of the twentieth and twenty-first centuries, voices whose moral fiber and clarity were forged in the crucible of war. They are, through their lived expertise, the authorities on the harm of war to the soul, the heart, the psyche, and the body of those who fight it.

Medicine that Heals

How do you know when you have begun healing from the trauma of war? For Lou, it was two months ago when he no longer "needed" to carry a gun. We first met at the Greenfield Y where exercise is the medicine that launched his journey to health, including reducing blood pressure, losing weight, and quelling diabetes. At his request, we met with Karen, his acupuncturist who, in her words, "brings soul and capacity to connect" to those she treats with holistic therapies.

"For a lot of my life after Vietnam," Lou explained, "I was depressed, bummed out. I had been in combat, came back with wounds, my head was messed up. The army showed no interest in my injuries," so he had to use political influence to get the US Department of Veterans Affairs, VA, to acknowledge that he had war-related injuries. "And all they did was give me a bunch of pills."

After returning from Vietnam, he worked as a respiratory therapist, then joined the state police and worked undercover in the narcotics division. "The job was ninety percent boredom and ten percent adrenalin," he said. "Until acupuncture, I was always in cop mode and carried a gun even after retiring." Thanks to the Y's Exercise is Medicine Program and acupuncture, he no longer takes pills. "I have my reflexes when I need them, but I've lost my paranoia. Since my acupuncture treatments, I don't have to carry a gun," he emphasized again—clearly his most significant sign of healing.

Shortly after our discussion, an article on the power of touch was published in the *New York Times*. The author, David Brooks, told the story of an Austrian orphanage in 1945 where infants received the best of nutrition and medical care, but in order to minimize contact with germs, they were not held or stroked. I imagined those little ones among the hundreds of thousands of orphans from World War II. Despite the best of physical care, a tragedy ensued. "Thirty-seven percent of the babies died before reaching age two," wrote Brooks.

Why did they fail to thrive? From infancy and throughout life, we flourish when we are loved and respected—often expressed as loving touch, respectful touch, and in conversation with others who listen and speak to us with eye contact and genuine interest. Lou's memories resonate with that. "When I came back from Vietnam, people shunned me. They asked stupid questions about combat. Vets could only talk to vets."

Healing wounds from war is less about painkillers and more about the curative power of listening, empathy, and respect in the treatment process, Karen explained. She described her life odyssey that led to her chosen practice with vets and first responders.

As a young woman, she was drawn to working with dying people and to children suffering trauma. After Hurricane Katrina, she treated homeless victims in New Orleans on "sidewalks, warehouses, anywhere" as part of Acupuncturists without Borders. Through her years of practicing acupuncture, she has "learned to listen with immense empathy, to speak from my heart. You need to bring soul and capacity to connect."

Lou gave a concrete picture of the effects: "After acupuncture, my whole demeanor does a 180 degree turn. It's like driving down Route 5/10 compared to Interstate 91 to the same destination."

"I do more meditation now," he added.

Our discussion left me with many converging streams of thought, the first involving the profound harm of war, beginning but not ending with vets. Our war veterans have among the highest rates of injury and pain, homelessness, divorce, suicide, and domestic violence.

As for the other victims of our wars, consider just one war. Some three million Vietnamese lost their lives during our war in Vietnam. Hundreds of thousands of mentally and physically handicapped children were born of parents exposed to the chemical warfare herbicide Agent Orange used by the US military. Another juxtaposing thought concerned the destructive power of exploitative touch, exposed in the Me Too movement, and my profound hope that that movement catalyzes a revolution in male behavior and accountability for their actions.

Finally, what of the path to peace in this world so that we do not have war orphans failing to thrive and war veterans with near permanent physical and spiritual wounds?

"Waging peace is never passive," writes Iraq war veteran-turned-peace-educator Paul Chappell. Training in peace literacy is as crucial as learning reading, writing, and mathematics, and it cannot be left only to parents, he warns. Schools must teach the history of strategic nonviolent campaigns that won civil rights and women's rights. They must teach the arts of listening, asking questions to achieve clarity and understanding, thus cultivating empathy and mutual communication, and the skills of disciplined resolution of conflict. As Gandhi affirmed, "If peace schooling were taken as seriously as military schooling, our world would be a much different place."

Frederick Douglass, the nineteenth-century African American activist to end slavery and win women's rights, so wisely said: "It is easier to raise a strong child than to heal a broken man."

Originally published February 12, 2018 in the *Greenfield Recorder*. Reprinted with permission.

Memorial Day:
Let Us Remember the Forgotten War Dead

May closes with Memorial Day, also called Decoration Day for the tradition of placing and planting flowers at the graves of war veterans. According to some sources, freed slaves began the tradition, when they gathered on May 1, 1865 in Charleston, West Virginia, to commemorate the death of Union soldiers. It was officially proclaimed on May 5, 1868 and observed with different customs in northern and southern states. President Woodrow Wilson extended Memorial Day to honor military dead from World War I and all future wars.

The national holiday, which honors soldiers who lost their lives in war, poses many complexities. Recalling President Abraham Lincoln's words in his Gettysburg address that "those who died shall not have died in vain," we recognize that Memorial Day does not distinguish, for example, between wars with a dimension of justice like the American Civil War and wars of aggression for control of natural resources like oil and geopolitical dominance, when young men and women lose their lives in vain. Who among us cannot name wars of the later twentieth- and early twenty-first centuries where our government's motives were ambiguous, hidden from the public, or based on deceit? "In war," the Greek playwright Aeschylus wrote, "truth is the first casualty."

Another dilemma of the national holiday to remember the military war dead is that many military war dead are excluded. After being pressured in 2012 by reporters investigating military suicides, the Veterans' Administration, VA, estimated that twenty-two soldiers per day were committing suicide, likely an underestimate because neither the VA nor the Pentagon had an accurate number nor maintained records on veterans who do not seek healthcare from the VA. That same year, more soldiers killed themselves than died fighting in Afghanistan. Thus, those killed in the midst of war are remembered honorably, but those who served side by side with them and died later from the unrelenting damage of war are forgotten.

Three recent wars exposed soldiers to chemical weapons and poisons that have consigned many to a slow death following years of illness and disability. The VA now associates heart disease, diabetes, neuropathy, Parkinson's disease, and a number of cancers suffered by Vietnam veterans as well as birth defects in their children to the veterans' exposure to the herbicide Agent Orange. However, it took veterans' advocates and their lawyers decades of confronting inept and corrupt government health studies and industry denial to overcome expedient myths and win VA health services and disability. Memorial Day does not encompass the military war dead who died after the war from exposure to chemical poisons on the battlefield.

More than thirty-five percent of 1991 Gulf War veterans suffer from a mysterious, multi-symptomatic illness termed Gulf War Syndrome including skin conditions; memory loss; and joint, respiratory, and GI tract problems which will likely shorten their lives. Studies to date suggest that exposures to depleted uranium, experimental vaccines, pesticides, and extremely toxic air pollution from burning oil wells and chemical burn pits during that war are the likely cause.

Some one thousand tons of radioactive depleted uranium, DU, were used by the US in the second war in Iraq to pierce metal tanks and concrete and steel structures, thus exposing soldiers and Iraqi citizens to radioactive dust and vapors after impact. Our country's decision to use DU in weapons was made in the context of intentional ignorance about the health risks to those exposed in conflict and post-conflict situations in Iraq.

Let us remember, then, on Memorial Day the men and women soldiers who have suffered and died from war-caused conditions called variably soldier's heart in the Civil War, shell shock in the First World War, PTSD in the Vietnam War, and moral injury in the Iraq War.

Let us not forget those who died from the nightmares of war—at their own hand. "The war is never over for those involved in it. It goes on for those damaged by it . . .," remarked a woman soldier assigned as a mortuary affairs specialist to handle maimed bodies of US soldiers killed by explosive devices in Afghanistan.

Let us remember all those veterans whose lives are foreshortened because of homelessness, unemployment, and the moral injury of war.

Perhaps we should inaugurate another memorial day to remember all the war dead and call it Day of Sorrow. By the end of the twentieth century, nine of ten who died in war were civilians not military, of which the majority were women and children. An epidemic of cancers and birth defects ravages Iraq since our two wars there. In Vietnam, third- and fourth-generation children born to mothers exposed to Agent Orange dioxin have severe mental and physical handicaps.

If we remember publicly all the dead and dying from war, as we do on Memorial Day for (some) military war dead, then perhaps the tragedy of the many, many millions of wasted lives, those who died in vain, would cry out—*war never again*.

Originally published May 13, 2015 at *ZCommunications*. Reprinted with permission.

World War I: Futility and Folly

Watching Londoners reveling in the streets on Armistice Day, November 11, 1918, the war critic and pacifist Bertrand Russell commented that people had cheered for war, then cheered for peace—"the crowd was frivolous still, and had learned nothing during the period of horror."

The first industrial war, World War I debuted poison gases, flamethrowers, aerial bombing, submarines, and machine guns, thus intensifying the scale of war wreckage and setting the norm for war in the twentieth century. World War I quickly became a total war moving inexorably toward total defeat of one combatant or the other with no political space nor will for early truce.

By policy, British war dead were not sent home lest the public turn against the war. Instead, they were buried in vast graveyards near battle sites in France and Belgium. Even today, Belgian and French farmers plowing fields in places of intense, interminable fighting and mass death on the Western Front unearth an estimated half million pounds of war detritus and soldiers' bones each year.

In Britain, a vast, unbreachable gap arose between war-ruined soldiers and war-fevered citizens suffused and infected with martial music, uniformed parades, and war propaganda—a chasm widened by pervasive government censoring of soldiers' mail. A pliant media shamelessly published false accounts that turned mass battle losses and defeats into victories. War-loyal British editors were rewarded with knighthood and peerage, and it was wryly noted that the war couldn't have lasted more than a month without the newspapers.

From the unyielding ugliness and butchery of World War I emerged soldier poets, notable among them Siegfried Sassoon and Wilfred Owen, whose unsparing style and content severed their work from the traditions of epic war poems and British romantic poetry. Living/dying in a trench war fraught with dead bodies and rats that fattened on them with rear guard commanders who sent battalions of teenage boys into the slaughter of machine-gun fire, the soldier poets castigated their homeland's war-mongering politicians and industrial profiteers.

The poets' sense of betrayal encompassed not only politicians securely giving war orders from home and complicit generals holed up in remote chateaus, but also citizens clamoring for war. Among them were patriotic mothers recruited to publicly shame unenlisted young men into joining and to heckle war resisters and pacifists. The war poets' realism countered—*but never superseded*—homeland novelists, artists, playwrights and poets, among them the empire-loving Rudyard Kipling, procured by the government to ennoble the war through facile appeals to patriotism and uniform, glory for country, and honor of serving.

Sassoon was initially lured by the romance and rousing propaganda of war and enlisted the first day. But he soon absorbed its fatal futility. He wrote of fellow soldiers doomed to die, with "dulled, sunken faces haggard and hopeless" whose obedient actions are "murdering the livid hours that grope for peace." The junior officer Wilfred Owens describes golden boys under his command turned into "hapless sacrificial victims" of an ugly, vast slaughter machine. Both poets drew from a reservoir of love and respect for the shared humanity of brother soldiers who, side by side with them, faced death with a noble courage, challenged death, and dared death face to face.

World War I soldiers had only each other in the face of death—a reality clarified by its soldier poets and writers—and incarnated in the 1914 Christmas truce spontaneously initiated by British, French, and German soldiers facing each other in trenches. Epic war poems from antiquity forward, hailing war as the penultimate expression of masculinity and mythic national greatness were displaced in the early twentieth-century war by simpler lyric poetry portraying war as solely generating the "wasteful heroic."

The German Veteran Voice

A word of command has made these silent figures our enemies; a word of command might transform them into our friends.
—Erich Maria Remarque

The unique camaraderie of war lingered also with novelist Erich Maria Remarque, who enlisted at nineteen in the World War I German army. He, too, admits bitterly that a sense of ideal and almost romantic war, propagated by the state's total propaganda campaign, turned high school boys into willing recruits for slaughter.

Some ten years after the war's end, Remarque published his first and what some consider the greatest antiwar novel, *All Quiet on the Western Front*. In subsequent novels, he continued to expose the ruination of war for those who fight in it and the willful deceit of those who incite it, mandate it, and seek stature from it. Remarque's nineteen-year-old soldier protagonist acutely observes the corrupt dynamics of war:

I see how peoples are set against each other foolishly, innocently, obediently slaying each other. While they—the promoters and boosters—continued to talk and write, we saw the wounded and dying. The wrong people do the fighting.

Of the educated class in countries at war, he observes that "the finest brains" are used to "invent weapons and words" to make war "yet more refined and enduring."

That siphoning of talented engineers and scientists for militarism became a modus operandi throughout the twentieth century of hot and cold wars. By some estimates, one third of all US engineering and science talent was employed in the military-industrial complex through the 1980s.

In perhaps the most incisive moment of Remarque's novel, a young German soldier gazes upon a young French soldier he has killed and ponders their common humanity with words that undercut the war's hard bitten hatred and national chauvinism.

Why do they never tell us that you are poor devils like us, that your mothers are just as anxious as ours, and that we have the same fear of death, and the same dying and the same agony.

All Quiet on the Western Front was banned in Nazi Germany.

War Is a Racket

"I spent thirty-three years in the marines, most of my time being a high-class muscle man for big business, for Wall Street and the bankers."

—Brigadier General Smedley Butler

War profiteering in World War I was mammoth, and no one nailed the profiteers and racketeers so head on as the straight-talking, be-medalled Brigadier General Smedley Butler. He describes his marine officer role in the early twentieth century as a "bully boy for American corporations," leading invasions into China, Nicaragua, Cuba, and Haiti on behalf of American banking, oil, and sugar interests. Later, during the Depression and Dust Bowl era, he became a staunch advocate for homeless and unemployed World War I veterans who had not yet received promised bonuses from the federal government. When those hapless veterans marched on Washington, Generals George S. Patton and Douglas MacArthur—of storied

World War II fame—called out the US Army, which burned their Hooverville shanties and attacked them brutally. Two people were killed, one an infant, and hundreds of veterans were injured.

Smedley Butler's most notable work is a pamphlet-like small book, *War Is a Racket*, written from the clear-eyed vantage of post-military life as war clouds again gathered over Europe. With unsparing prose, he assails the war industries for the blood on their hands—for fomenting war abroad and securely pocketing its profits at home—as bracingly as any ardent pacifist. He cites the gunpowder giant DuPont whose fortunes increased nearly ten-fold during World War I and General Chemical Company whose wartime profits soared by 1,400 percent. Leather, boot-making, garment and metals industries, airplane, engine and ship builders—all the outfitters of armed conflict—enjoyed immense profit.

Making the world safe for democracy: Woodrow Wilson's mantra sold US entry into the war to a public that had reelected him in 1916 to stay out of war. Butler describes Wilson employing the same tactics used so thoroughly in Britain and Germany: shaming young men not yet in uniform, jailing pacifists, severe erosion of civil liberties, enlisting film stars and clergy to assure that God is on "our" side, and producing xenophobic propaganda.

As Butler saw it, war is first and foremost about making the world safe for war profits. It is the oldest, most profitable racket, he declares, one in which billions of dollars are made for millions of lives destroyed. Of the estimated fifty-two-billion-dollar cost of World War I, industry war profiteers pocketed nearly one-third. More than twenty-one thousand new American millionaires and billionaires emerged from the human ashes of the war while the federal government was mired in post-war debt, a debt paid for by working people's taxes.

Little has changed regarding Butler's stinging analysis except that war industry profits have grown and with them the national budget for militarism. Given the sacred cow status of the military entitlement program within the federal budget, a palpable difference between wartime and so-called peacetime economies no longer exists.

In 2011, 27 cents of every federal tax dollar went to military expenses while 2.5 cents, 1.9 cents, and 1.2 cents respectively supported education, energy and environment, and international affairs. That calculation does not include associated costs of war such as veterans' benefits, reconstruction in Iraq and Afghanistan, assistance to allies, interest on war-related debt, impact of Iraq war on the cost of oil, and so on. Further, one of two primary drivers of the current federal budget deficit is the wars in Afghanistan and Iraq, the other being Bush and more recently Trump tax cuts. As of 2020, the war on terror has added $2.4 trillion to the national debt.

Toll of War

The Sinister Spirit sneered: "It had to be!"
And again the Spirit of Pity whispered, "Why?"

—Thomas Hardy

World War I, if anything, was an immense and complex setback for democracy. In his acclaimed chronicle of the war and its resisters, *To End All* Wars, Adam Hochschild collates direct and indirect death, injury, enmities, and poisonous legacies of that total war. He concludes that between 8.5 and 9.5 million soldiers overall were killed, 21 million were wounded, including many mangled and disfigured, and between 12 million and 13 million civilians died.

Elevated rates of suicide followed the war, according to Hochschild, and the war triggered Turkish genocide of Armenians, replicated on much larger scale a generation later by Germany against European Jews. He also states that the war also triggered the Russian civil war with fatalities of between seven and ten million. Four hundred thousand African laborers, forced to carry war supplies by colonial powers, died from disease and from being worked to death, according to Hochschild. Their death rate was higher than that of British soldiers. Hundreds of thousands of African women and children—all victims of the empires at war— died from famine resulting from theft of animals and grains by rival European armies.

Europe's landscape and land resources were ravaged: Germans in retreat employed scorched earth policy in Belgium and France.

Russians did the same in retreating from the Eastern Front. Unexploded shells in Belgium and France in areas of intense, prolonged fighting along the Western Front continue to kill. French bomb demolition specialists destroy an average of nine hundred tons of the war's ordnance per year, a hazardous occupation that has killed hundreds of such specialists. Patches of untouched forest and scrub carry perimeter signs warning hikers to avoid those areas containing live shells.

Massive government propaganda campaigns on all sides engendered a deep cynicism after the war and contributed to public dismissal of early rumors about German death camps.

Total, industrial war broke through the limits of what many Europeans thought morally permissible in war against other white Europeans, and it seasoned warring countries for conducting atrocities in future wars. Germany torpedoed neutral ships. Both sides used chemical warfare, which presaged Agent Orange in Vietnam. The British blockaded Germany to starve the country into submission. Cities were bombed from the air, which would be replicated and augmented to extreme levels in World War II, culminating in Hiroshima and Nagasaki.

The 1918 flu pandemic, which killed fifty million people worldwide, spread more rapidly by enormous numbers of troops on the move.

Armistice was declared on November 11, 1918 with the stipulation that hostilities along the Western Front would stop at eleven in the morning French time. Even so, soldiers on both sides continued shelling each other throughout the day—such is the vengeful habit of a long, grinding war, a reflex not yet entrenched in the teenage soldiers of the 1914 Christmas truce who laid down arms and played soccer together like friends and brothers.

The Paris Peace Conference began in January, 1919, and lasted the year, with the victors dividing the spoils of war, redrawing the defeated empires' boundaries, devising conditions for a treaty with Germany and the Austro-Hungarian and Ottoman empires, and designing a doomed international body, the League of Nations, to mediate future disputes between nations. Countries from Finland to

Czechoslovakia emerged from fragmented European empires. The Ottoman Empire in the Middle East was parceled out, with three provinces opportunistically patched together as the new British protectorate of Iraq. German colonies in the Pacific and Africa were divided among the winners. High-minded Allied rhetoric about self-determination of European peoples was not applied to African or Asian colonies or to oil-rich Arab territories.

The Treaty of Versailles to end the war was forged by the Allies and signed by a reluctant Germany on June 28, 1919. It established the reduction of German territory and German disarmament. It also required Germany to make huge reparation payments and formally admit guilt for starting the war. The punitive peace treaty has been widely described as sowing the seeds of World War II "The tragedies of the future [were] written into it as if by the devil's own hand," stated historian-diplomat George Kennan.

The Folly of War

In December of 1916, Woodrow Wilson offered to negotiate a "peace without victory" among the warring powers. Millions of soldiers had died for advances or retreats measured in meters of land along the Western Front while Germans were surviving on potatoes and conscripting children fifteen years of age. Yet, no side was willing to agree to a settlement that would forfeit them some prize for the sacrifice in lives, including financial reparations—given the near bankrupting cost of the war. Further, a stalemated peace without victory would likely instigate popular revolt against the throne or government, the military caste, the landowners, industrialists, and barons of business in all countries drawn into war.

"Only a war of gain offered any hope of their survival in power," notes historian Barbara Tuchman in her epic analysis of war from Troy to Vietnam, *The March of Folly*. Even revolution in the loser's country was feared by the Allies because of its infectious nature. Thus, at the end of the war, World War I victors would leave machine guns in an otherwise demilitarized Germany for the government to quell burgeoning socialist protests.

Tuchman contrasts the punitive winners-take-all Treaty of Versailles with the "peace without victory" proposed by Wilson.

And, she speculates, "For the world, the alternative would have changed history; no victory, no reparations, no war guilt, no Hitler, possibly no Second World War."

Imagine

After a week of travel along the Western Front and walking among miles of cemeteries for British, Belgian, French, and other soldiers killed in war, Hochschild finds a lone, out of the way plot with a large cross and a dozen small ones honoring the 1914 Christmas truce spontaneously celebrated by soldiers on both sides. He notes that the modest memorial was near where they had played soccer together and that on one of the small crosses someone had carved the word "imagine."

And thus prompted, he imagines another cemetery filled with the thousands of war critics, pacifists, and conscientious objectors from Britain, Germany, and the United States and the thousands of soldiers and sailors on all sides who mutinied, refused to fight, or simply left the front over the war's futility and folly. "This would be a cemetery," he wrote, "of those who often knew in advance they were going to lose yet felt the pacifist fight was worth it anyway, because of the example it set for those who might one day win."

Originally published November 11, 2012 at *Truthout*. Reprinted with permission.

The Iraq War and Moral Injury

The cycle of violence that began with the US invasion now permeates every aspect of society. The daily reality of living in US-occupied Iraq is so grim it's beyond the comprehension of most Americans.

—Salam Talib in
Winter Soldier Iraq and Afghanistan:
Eyewitness Accounts of the Occupations

On March 20, 2003, the United States launched a mammoth aerial bombardment of missiles and bombs on Baghdad in what then Secretary of Defense Donald Rumsfeld gleefully described as a "shock and awe" onslaught the world had never seen. The war was expected to be brief, surgically smart, and victorious. It was none of those.

By 2008, up to a million Iraqis had died from war-induced violence. Most were civilians. At least one-sixth of the Iraqi people became internally displaced with war refugees fleeing to other parts of the country and to nearby countries.

More than 4,000 American soldiers were killed and 32,000 wounded—many with serious brain and spinal injuries. Up to thirty percent of Iraq War veterans treated by the Veterans' Administration have PTSD, with higher rates among those veterans deployed multiple times. By 2010, full US costs of the debt-financed war, including long-term care and disability for veterans, extortionist private military contractors, increased oil prices and impacts on the US economy, were estimated to be 3 trillion US dollars. Between 2002 and 2009, the cost of war was one of the two biggest factors in the ballooning federal deficit. By late 2019 the costs rose to 6.4 trillion US dollars.

On December 15, 2011, the United States marked the formal end of combat operations in Iraq with vastly divergent assessments of the nearly nine-year war. At the closing military ceremony in Iraq, General Ray Odierno drew forth America's narcissistic self-image as the force of global liberation: "The war was for the shared ideals of freedom, liberty, and justice."

Former Deputy Secretary of Defense Paul Wolfowitz, who held the office from 2001-2005, an architect of the Iraq War, penned an upbeat, self-vindicating take for the *New York Times* on how we left Iraq as a cleansed country with the potential to become another South Korea as the engine of political and economic progress in the Middle East. And, he adds, at a bargain of collateral damage compared to the Korean War. He showed his hand in suggesting that we need to maintain a long-term military presence there because abandoning Iraq completely would harm US interests in the region and beyond. In fact, neoconservative strategists had identified Iraq as the key to control of the Middle East and its resources in the early 1990s for the grand post-Cold War scheme of American world dominance.

For Iraqis, the war left their country in ruins and a humanitarian disaster. Baghdad ranked last in a May 2010 international study of most livable cities because of the destruction of power and sewage treatment plants, factories, schools, hospitals, and museums. Iraq ranked last among 144 countries on the 2009 Global Peace Index and seventh worst of 177 countries on the 2010 Failed State Index. The country's natural resources are "mortgaged for the next fifty years to the international oil contractors."

Roots of War

Why the war against Iraq, when we were already at war in Afghanistan as we pursued the mastermind of September 11? The reasons changed like a chameleon does color: first, to eliminate non-existent weapons of mass destruction; next, because the tyrant Saddam Hussein might support terrorists; then, to herald democracy in Iraq. When state-building by gunpoint and bombing failed, we occupied Iraq to stabilize the country we had destabilized.

The Bush-Cheney cabal called it a preemptive war against a grave threat, and the mainstream US press dutifully published from the Administration's playbook, whipping up American patriotism and war-fever. In the momentum to war, respected US diplomats, among them Colonel Ann Wright, resigned over the illegality of the war, and US and British whistleblowers leaked evidence of cherry-picked facts and misinformation retrofitted to predetermined war policy–all to no avail in Washington and London.

When the Bush administration failed to win UN Security Council approval for war against Iraq, it cobbled together a coalition of the willing to give a multinational patina to a thoroughly US-driven war. Except for Britain, which colluded in the war, the *coalition of the coerced* as Phyllis Bennis incisively called it consisted of countries dependent on American arms, arms training, aid, trade, and security.

Based on shreddable lies, as the case for war in Iraq was, much of the world knew it to be a war of aggression–*the supreme international crime*. In the buildup to the war, the global chorus opposing it reached a crescendo on February 15 when more than twelve million people in six hundred cities on five continents marched and demonstrated in solidarity. The size, the scale, and the timing– before war began–of that *"No to War"* protest was unprecedented in human history.

International security analyst Michael Klare has collated five supporting facts to foreground the oil motive behind the Iraq War. Iraq has the second largest supply of oil in the world—ten-percent of global supply and large untapped reservoirs, Klare notes. In late 2001, the state department convened the working group on oil and energy consisting of expatriate Iraqi oil managers to plan the privatization of Iraqi oil after regime change in Baghdad. US oil companies also met with ex-pat Iraqi oil managers to discuss their role in privatizing Iraqi oil.

In the war planning, a special military task force was created to protect oil fields once the invasion commenced, the first ground action involving US Navy Sea, Air, and Land Teams, and US Navy SEALS, seizing Iraq's offshore oil facilities, Klare observes. Onshore, as missiles and bombs demolished Baghdad's infrastructure and the city's museums and treasures were being plundered on a scale that scholars of antiquity deemed an irredeemable loss of human culture, US military solely safeguarded the oil ministry in Baghdad.

Military Dissidents, Critics, Activists, and Voices:
A Moral Tenor

Iraq war soldiers fought in a war embedded with a post-Vietnam US media determined to treat soldiers as patriotic warriors and heroes no matter the baseless claims and venal motives of the war. Even so, thousands of those soldiers turned against the war and declared themselves conscientious objectors, went away without leave or AWOL, refused to deploy, risked prison, published on blogs, spoke out, and returned their War-on-Terror medals in a public act of conscience. Some spoke of seeing their children's faces in the faces of terrified Iraqi children and others, of being changed by witnessing the crushing grief of Iraqis losing loved ones to American bullets. *Their voices have a uniquely moral tenor.*

Moral Injury

As a marine, Ross Caputi dropped bombs in the second siege of Al-Fallujah during a November-December overkill assault that left thousands of civilians dead, caused hundreds of thousands of war refugees, reduced the city to rubble, and poisoned its environment with depleted uranium and heavy metals from weapons and ammunition. Today Fallujah has an epidemic of children born with horrific birth defects and leukemia, both war-linked health tragedies that the US military denies and the major US media would not touch. Caputi has written publicly of his sorrow and regret for his role in Fallujah.

The veterans "who fought there," Caputi contends, "still do not understand who they fought against or what they were fighting for." They were concurrently "the iron fist of American empire" and "an expendable loss in the eyes of their leaders." A country that launches a war of aggression and calls its soldiers heroes for killing innocent people turned by war propaganda into enemies "has reversed the roles of aggressor and defender, moralized the immoral, and shaped our society's present understanding of war," he contends.

Samantha Schutz deployed to Iraq as an army journalist. Quickly, she said, she felt like "a propagandist." She was ordered to "put a positive spin" on her war reports and to avoid negative incidents and stories. In feeding news to embedded journalists from the West, she discloses "we censored what they were allowed to see, experience, write about, or film." When she could no longer in conscience deceive the American public about the war in her reports, she went AWOL while on leave and then, willing to face the consequences, turned herself in to the military. "I can honestly say that I would rather have spent the three years I have left on my contract in a cell than serving the military organization," she said. She was discharged from the Army and denied veterans' benefits.

As a member of Bravo Company 2-16, Ethan McCord rescued two injured children from a van in Baghdad. American helicopter gunners had riddled it with bullets. The children's father, having stopped to help a group of Iraqi men and international reporters gunned down in the airstrike, was also killed. The video of that massacre, *Collateral Damage*, was leaked to Wikileaks by Private Bradley (later Chelsea) Manning. Later, McCord and fellow soldier Josh Stieber published "An Open Letter of Reconciliation and Responsibility to the Iraqi People" where they acknowledged that, as soldiers, they contributed to the pain of the Iraqi people and to their community's pain and to the death and injury of their loved ones by occupying their country.

Their letter concludes.

With such pain, friendship might be too much to ask. Please accept our apology, our sorrow, our care, and our dedication to change from the inside out. We are doing what we can to speak out against the wars and military policies responsible for what happened to you and your loved ones. Our hearts are open to hearing how we can take steps *to support you through the pain that we have caused.*

Both McCord and Stieber have since worked in efforts of reparation and reconciliation with Iraqi Health Now, which provides direct medical and health aid to people in Iraq.

Returning Medals

In May 2012, forty-one years after Vietnam veterans hurled medals, ribbons, and discharge papers at the US Capitol Building in Washington, nearly fifty uniformed members of Iraq Veterans Against the War did the same in Chicago. They led tens of thousands of protestors from across the country. A group of Afghan women joined them in a march as participants chanted "No NATO, no war. We don't kill for you. No more."

At police barricades that separated them from NATO generals and politicians summiting about the future of Afghanistan, each veteran spoke about why they were returning their global war on terror medals and war ribbons. And each then turned and hurled the medals toward the NATO summit.

US Army Sergeant Allejandro Villatoro opened the speak out and others picked up the theme:

Some of us killed innocents. Some of us helped in continuing these wars from home. Some of us watched our friends die. Some of us are not here, because we took our own lives. We did not get the care promised to us by our government. All of us watched failed policies turn into bloodshed. Listen to us, hear us, and think: was any of this worth it?"

My name is Jason Hurd. I spent ten years in the United States Army as a combat medic. I deployed to Baghdad in 2004. I'm here to return my Global War on Terrorism Service Medal in solidarity with the people of Iraq and the people of Afghanistan.

I am deeply sorry for the destruction that we have caused in those countries and around the globe. I am proud to stand on this stage with my fellow veterans and my Afghan sisters. These were lies. I'm giving them back.

My name is Shawna, and I was a nuclear biological chemical specialist for a war that didn't have any weapons of mass destruction. So I deserted. I'm one of forty thousand people that left the United States Armed Forces because this is a lie!

My name is Zach LaPorte, and I'm an Iraq war veteran from Milwaukee, Wisconsin. I'm giving back my medals today because I feel like I was duped into an illegal war that was sold to me on the guise that I was going to be liberating the Iraqi people, when instead of liberating the people, I was liberating their oil fields.

My name's Nate. I served in the US Navy from 1999 to 2003 and participated in the invasions of Iraq and Afghanistan. I was wrong to sign myself up for that. I apologize to the Iraqi and Afghani people for destroying your countries.

My name is Aaron Hughes. I served in the Illinois Army National Guard from 2000 to 2006. This medal right here is for Anthony Wagner. He died in 2011. This medal right here is for the one-third of the women in the military that are sexually assaulted by their peers. We talk about standing up for our sisters—we talk about standing up for our sisters in Afghanistan, and we can't even take care of our sisters here. And this medal right here is because I'm sorry. I'm sorry to all of you. I'm sorry.

Having no medals, Mary Kirkland carried the military photograph of her son, army infantryman Derek Kirkland, to leave with the discarded medals. He had been haunted by killing other human beings in Iraq, and in despair, he committed suicide. A fellow soldier acknowledged that after previous suicide attempts, Derek's commanders bullied him, calling him "sissy" and "pussy."

"My son was the victim of a needless war," Kirkland said, "and we are still doing that to the Afghan people and doing it to our troops. It is the innocent dying."

The Price of War

In the third week of December 2011, remaining occupying US troops in Iraq were withdrawn unceremoniously in a fortified concrete courtyard with only a small band playing as the US flag was furled. Defense Secretary Leon Panetta avowed that the price was high, but the US invasion and occupation "gave birth to an independent, free, and sovereign Iraq."

Iraq Prime Minister al-Maliki did not attend.

In contrast to the discreet exit President Barack Obama welcomed returning US troops at Fort Bragg with big braggadocios and tired conceits of American military altruism. The war was "one of the most extraordinary chapters in American military history." Having sacrificed so much for "people they never met," the returning soldiers are part of what makes "us special as Americans." Unlike other empires, which wage war for resources and territory, "We do it because it's right," Obama said.

The same week, Yanar Mohammed, founding director of the Organization of Women's Freedom in Iraq, OWFI, was interviewed on the condition of Iraq as the American occupation ended. She described Iraqi cities full of destroyed buildings and broken streets with intermittent electricity and unsafe drinking water. Iraq, she said, had become a country of ninety percent poor and one percent rich living in the Green Zone, burdened with the most corrupt government in the world that is giving control of the Iraqi people's oil resources to multinational oil companies.

Iraqi women "are the biggest losers" in the war, Mohammed asserted, ending with women's extreme lack of freedom, lack of social security, lack of opportunity, and increased sexual terror. She asserted that the current generation of girls would grow up less literate than their mothers—reversing the tide of human development.

Mohammed's organization has conducted extensive high-risk investigations into the prevalence and plight of Iraqi widows, women, and girls kidnapped and killed and women trafficked into prostitution. By 2006, OWFI had observed an "epidemic rise" in the number of women prostituted in brothels, workplaces, and hideouts in Baghdad. Through covert investigation, they learned of the trafficking of women within Iraq for Iraqi men and for members of the US military as well as for residents in nearby countries. Democracy in Iraq has been crushed for women, according to Mohammed and OWFI. American women soldiers in Iraq were big losers, also. Nearly two hundred thousand US women served there in as dangerous situations as men. Though barred from combat, they carried machine guns as they patrolled streets, served as gunners on vehicles, dismantled explosives, drove trucks down bomb-ridden streets, and rescued the dead and injured in battle zones. The same women found themselves concurrently caught in a second, *more damaging* war–a private one in the barracks.

As one female soldier put it, "They basically assume that because you are a girl in the army, you're obligated to have sex with them." An estimated one in three active-duty woman is sexually assaulted. Nearly all report constant sexual harassment.

In another key event, the state department released the National Action Plan, NAP, on Women, Peace, and Security on December 19, 2011, championed by then Secretary of State Hilary Clinton. NAP brings the United States into compliance with UN resolutions that call for integrating women as full partners in conflict resolution and peace building. Its purpose is to assure that US diplomatic, defense, and development policies are gauged in part by their impact on women in countries where we engage diplomatically, militarily, and economically. One example of implementing NAP would be to "strengthen protection for women and girls in conflict situations, with greater focus on greater legal accountability for rape and sexual violence."

Tragically, our diplomatic and defense policies in Iraq created the opposite: conditions where up to two million widows are penniless, legions of women were killed by fundamentalists squads in Basra, thousands have ended up in prostitution, and Sharia law holding in part that women are legally worth half of what men are worth and socially worth a quarter of what men are worth, is embedded within the new constitution–a potential setback of more than fifty years.

The same war has left tens of thousands of American women soldiers broken physically, mentally, and spiritually from military sexual trauma instigated by fellow soldiers. Having the fortitude to acknowledge publicly that women are "the biggest losers" in our vainglorious militarist policies in Iraq, Afghanistan, and elsewhere would give substance and integrity to the National Action Plan on Women, Peace, and Security.

Originally published March 29, 2013 at *Truthout*. Reprinted with permission.

Burn Pits Violate All Health and Environmental Standards

The Burn Pits
by Joseph Hickman
Hot Books. 2016

They are called this generation's Agent Orange—the open fire pits operated on more than 230 US military bases across Iraq and Afghanistan during our wars there. Every kind of waste—from plastics, batteries, old ordnance, asbestos, pesticide containers, and tires to biomedical, chemical, and nuclear waste to dead animals, human waste, body parts, and corpses—was incinerated in them.

The word incinerate misleads, however, suggesting an enclosed burning facility with pollution controls. The barbaric burn pits were dug on military bases in the midst of housing, work, and dining facilities without any pollution controls. Tons of waste—an average of ten pounds daily per soldier—burned in them every day, all day and all night, blackening the air and coating clothing, beds, desks, and dining halls with ash laden with hundreds of toxins and carcinogens. Burn pits recklessly violated US Environmental Protection Agency and Department of Defense waste disposal regulations. Predictably, base commanders temporarily shut them down when politician and high-ranking generals visited the bases.

Even more perilous, some US bases were built on remnants of Iraqi military bases bombed and flattened by US air strikes. A handful of those bases—at least five—had contained stockpiles of old chemical warfare weapons, among them the nerve agent sarin and the blistering agent mustard gas. American military base burn pits were placed and dug within the chemical weapons residues without a single soil sample taken.

In his no-holds-barred book, *The Burn Pits: the Poisoning of America's Soldiers*, former marine and army sergeant Joseph Hickman exposes the knowing contamination of thousands of soldiers stationed on bases with the lethal pits. After interviewing more than a thousand very sick veterans and military contractors about their exposures and investigating the non response of the Pentagon, high-ranking military in Iraq and Afghanistan, and the Veterans Health Administration, the author concludes,

In my experience as a noncommissioned officer, and after serving twenty years in the military, I can honestly say I would believe the words of a private over a general any day of the week.

The tragic tale of burn pit victims replicates the bitter chronicles of Vietnam War veterans' exposure to Agent Orange, the ongoing "Gulf War Syndrome," and depleted uranium exposure, from all of which hundreds of thousands of veterans are injured and disabled. Further, some exposed veterans were likely victims of the epidemic of military sexual assault in the Iraq and Afghanistan wars. Yet, those victimized by those crushing maladies have been ignored, disbelieved, blamed for their plight, and refused help by their government. Such veterans tell an *inconvenient truth* that yields, at best, years of often inconsequential study by a reluctant government, a government that will spend hundreds of billions each fiscal year on defense industries and weapons of war but penny pinches for its injured veterans.

A final word on the ultimate war victims. The people of Iraq have been multiply poisoned from our initial 1991 war there through the war on ISIS. The arc of poisons begins with the oil fires in Kuwait that burned for seven months after being set by fleeing Iraqi soldiers and depleted uranium used by the US in the 1991 first Gulf War and in the 2003-2011 Iraq War. And it extends to burn pit air toxins from US bases that wafted into nearby towns and cities and recent oil conflagrations set by ISIS and ignited during US bombing of ISIS strongholds.

Once among the best health systems in the Middle East, Iraq's system of care has been decimated by war. Its health facilities destroyed and not rebuilt, and doctors have fled the incessant violence. Massive civilian suffering is unrelieved with severe shortages of medicines, unsafe drinking water, a broken government, millions dead or displaced by twenty-five years of war, and the surge of fundamentalist subjugation of women, especially since the Iraq War. The startling rise of birth defects and cancers in Iraq and high lead levels in baby teeth of Iraqi children are, in large part, the legacy of our war-created pollution in that country.

We, the United States, have never fixed what we have broken in war, with the exception of the Marshall Plan in white Western

Europe after World War II. Our imperial ambitions lie at the core of many now ruined countries, millions of dead across the world, millions of living dead and displaced, toxic environments, and hundreds of thousands of disabled US veterans who fought for the war machine. In the words of economist Jeffrey Sachs, "It's time to abandon the reveries, burdens, and self-deceptions of empire and invest in development at home and in partnership with the rest of the world."

Originally published 2015 in the *Veteran Magazine V V A G*. Reprinted with permission.

Beatitudes for War Veterans,
War Victims and Military Families

Blessed is the veteran of World War I, who spent his life exposing the horrors of war for those who fight in it and the willful deceit of those who declare it and seek stature from it. In his first antiwar novel, Erich Maria Remarque wrote:

I see how peoples are set against each other foolishly, innocently, obediently slaying each other while they, the promoters and boosters of war, continued to talk and write, we saw the wounded and dying. The wrong people do the fighting.

His book, *All Quiet on the Western Front*, was banned in Nazi Germany.

Blessed are the children of veterans who break the code of silence on *the war that never ends*: living with the "attendant nightmares" of their veteran fathers and being "the objects of their war-ridden rage and war-honed violence." *War Is Not Over When It's Over* chronicles, through interviews and photos, the spill over of brutal violence against girls and women in six war-ruined countries. The author Ann Jones's own life was "darkened by war." Her thrice-decorated WWI-veteran father turned his war-fed anger and violence on her and her mother.

Blessed is the World War II combat veteran who turned his revulsion at the racism of boot camp and the brutality of war into a life of nonviolent activism for civil rights and radical witness for peace. Philip Berrigan believed "there will be no healing for veterans until we disavow war completely, until we disarm the bomb and the killing machine and ourselves." His lifelong question: "Can I remedy my violence, can I heal myself until I try to heal the body of humankind from the curse of war?"

Blessed is the writer Anonymous for her courage in exposing a taboo subject: The mass rape of an estimated hundred thousand women in Berlin—of which she was one—by conquering Russian soldiers over a period of seven weeks and the mass rejection of those women as shameless and besmirched by returning German men emasculated by defeat. Anonymous's book, *A Woman in Berlin*, was rejected by German publishers and only published years later in the United States. The author did not reveal her name because of fear of threats and reprisals.

Blessed is the daughter of two hibakusha, the shunned Japanese survivors of atomic bombs, who has assumed the mantle of speaking out against nuclear weapons and for world peace. The bombs scarred her parents both mentally and physically. Her father lashed out and her mother withdrew into depression. "For me," says Miyako Taguchi, founder of the organization Hibakusha Stories from Hiroshima and Nagasaki to Future Generations, "I always live with the effects, the reality of the bomb, and the modern arsenals of more than twenty-seven thousand nuclear weapons. No matter who has them, we are all their victims."

Blessed are all the veterans against wars, current and past, and those who have returned to the countries and peoples they harmed to make reparation. *Blessed are the Veterans for Peace* who walked in rural Maine to bear witness to the human tragedy that recent wars have caused for local villages, towns, and families, including unprecedented rates of suicide among soldiers who served in the Afghanistan and Iraq wars and the many suffering from war-related PTSD, head trauma, and sexual assault.

Blessed are the women veterans who have broken the silence about sexual abuse of women in the military and the minefields they traverse in disclosing it. Army combat veteran Robynn Murray, sexually assaulted during military training and suffering PTSD from the trauma of war in Iraq, testifies that women fight another war inside the military, a war of rape and sexual abuse. *Blessed are those veterans* who have chosen the righteous path of truth telling about a military more intent on shielding the warrior culture from scandal than on protecting the one in three women soldiers who are sexually assaulted.

Blessed are the Military Families Against the War who have called loudly for an end to the wars in Afghanistan and Iraq and for recognition of the exorbitant costs of those wars to our country. *Blessed is the mother, Cindy Sheehan,* who upon learning of her soldier son's death in Iraq was reborn as a world citizen, a woman who knows that the human family is worth struggling for for the rest of her life.

Blessed are the September 11 Families for Peaceful Tomorrows, a core of two hundred family members directly affected by loss on September 11, 2001 who have turned their grief into action for peace. They opposed the bombing of Afghanistan as a response to their loved ones' deaths, raised funds to be distributed to Afghan families affected by US military action, and documented their first trip to Afghanistan in the educational film *Civilian Casualties.*

Originally published November 11, 2010 online at *Buzzflash.com.* Reprinted with permission.

Nuclear Power: A Wolf in Sheep's Clothing

Nuclear power was purposely cast as "Atoms for Peace" by the administration of President Dwight D. Eisenhower to dissociate it from the dread of nuclear weapons felt by many countries after the United States bombing of Hiroshima and Nagasaki in August 1945. In the halcyon days of the 1950s, US acolytes of the Atoms for Peace program aspired to building one thousand nuclear power reactors to generate the country's electricity.

With ninety-four nuclear power reactors at present operating in fifty-six nuclear power plants, the US has the largest number of any country in the world, a number that conclusively deflates early technocentric optimism. The nuclear plant Vogtle Units 3 and 4 in Georgia, forecast to open in 2021 and 2022 respectively, would be the first new nuclear reactors coming on line in our country since 1990.

Since the year 2000, a sought-after nuclear renaissance has fizzled. Why the failed future of nuclear power? Countless reasons:

- high building costs and long timelines for construction and permitting—between 7.7 and 10 years versus from 2 to 5 years for solar and wind
- potential for catastrophic accidents and contamination: think Three-Mile Island, Chernobyl, and Fukushima, where millions of tons of radioactive groundwater have leaked into the Pacific Ocean
- cancer risks from mining, milling, processing of uranium, and plant operation: no safe level of radiation exposure, according to the National Academy of Sciences in 2006

- radioactive waste, some lasting for millennia, with no safe, permanent disposal solution in sight
- risks to nuclear-power-plant functioning from climate crisis: fiercer hurricanes, flooding, fire, and drought
- carbon footprint: six times that of wind and two times that of solar
- potential target for terrorists
- risk of nuclear weapons proliferation from spent fuel
- depleted uranium, DU, a waste product from refining uranium for nuclear power plants, recycled into toxic weapons of war
- rising costs of nuclear power vs. plummeting prices of solar and wind per kilowatt-hour, and
- antinuclear power activism throughout the country

The Connecticut River Valley spawned a vibrant non-violent resistance movement against nuclear power in the 1970s that inspired the country. The many historic markers of antinuclear activism include the iconic 1974 toppling of a nuclear power research weather tower on the Montague Plains in western Massachusetts by a young, intrepid Sam Lovejoy; the massive 1977 Clamshell Alliance protests against building the Seabrook, New Hampshire nuclear power plant; and antinuclear activist Anna Gyorgy's 1979 handbook *No Nukes: everyone's guide to nuclear power*.

More recently, the successful campaign to shutter Vermont Yankee nuclear power plant in Vernon, Vermont, in 2014 was achieved by tireless, networking activists including many Vermonters and thirty or more women of the Shut It Down Affinity Group, among hundreds of others. Declining profits helped accelerate the closure.

The cradle-to-grave campaign against nuclear power continues with Deb Katz and the Citizen Awareness Network, CAN. CAN tracks and exposes joint corporate and Congressional legislative efforts to transport high-level nuclear waste to Latino communities of West Texas and the southeast corner of New Mexico. A grave environmental injustice is being perpetrated by choosing to turn poor, powerless communities into nuclear wastelands and sacrifice zones for nuclear-power waste from the rest of the country.

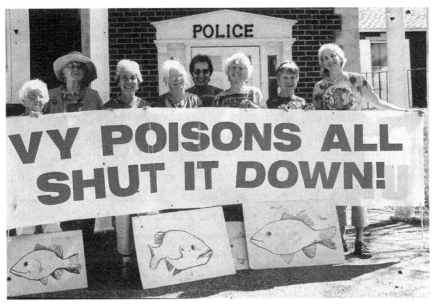

The Shut-It-Down Affinity Group crossed the line at Vermont Yankee some forty-seven times from 2005 to 2013 in an effort to close the Vernon, Vermont, nuclear power plant. Frances Crowe, Nancy First, Hattie Nestel, Paki Wieland, Mary-Ann DeVita Palmieri, Sandra Boston, Ellen Graves, and Betsy Corner, from left, are among more than thirty-five women who acted with the group shown outside the Vernon Police Station.

photo copyright by Marcia Gagliardi

In decline, the nuclear power industry desperately markets itself as clean energy—*a wolf in sheep's clothing,* as the following articles expose. President Barack Obama fell for it as did Donald J. Trump, who also baptized so-called *clean coal.* And now the Biden/Harris administration retains nuclear power in its so-called clean energy mix, in an otherwise well-received climate plan. As nuclear critic and blogger Paul Gipe expounds, "clean energy is one of those misleading words that party leaders and, importantly, fundraisers can use to elicit money from donors of all stripes."

But a new finding may just sound the death knell for nuclear power and the clean energy myth. In October 2020, a study of 125 countries over a span of 25 years found that those that had set their future energy course solely in renewable technologies have lowered their carbon-based greenhouse gas emissions significantly more than countries with a mix of nuclear and renewables.

The following articles were published between 2011 and 2016, a span of years in which world news foregrounded the extreme risks of nuclear power. The 2011 Fukushima Daiichi, Japan, nuclear power plant disaster was caused by the Tōhoku earthquake and tsunami. Tragic consequences included the meltdown of three radioactive cores, an explosion and release of radioactivity to the air, and ongoing radioactive contamination of groundwater and the Pacific Ocean.

Fukushima was the most severe nuclear accident since the Chernobyl, Ukraine, disaster in 1986, when a nuclear reactor exploded and released massive amounts of radioactive material into the environment. Air contamination with radioactive dust is ongoing today at Chernobyl. Fukushima provoked memories and reflection on Chernobyl and catalyzed intense activist organizing aimed at shutting down aging nuclear reactors, among them Vermont Yankee and Diablo Canyon in California.

Given that the following articles document crisis events, debates, and activism of that unique period of nuclear disaster and extreme contamination, I have left them intact in their time frame, 2011-2016, concluding with an update on the Fukushima nuclear power plant meltdown in 2011.

Eisenhower and the Road Not Taken:
A Cautionary Tale for Obama

Throughout January 2011, a suite of overlapping articles has extolled President Dwight D. Eisenhower's prescience about the "continuing imperative" of disarmament, the rise since World War II of a "permanent war-based industry dictating national policy," and the need for citizen vigilance and engagement to curb the "military-industrial" and Congressional complex. In his brief January 1961 farewell address, the two-term president Eisenhower also warned of the undue influence of the scientific-technological elite and their quest for singular, silver bullets to cure every ill; of the loss of independent intellectual pursuit in "the free university" with the rise of government research grants; and of mortgaging the future by overconsuming finite resources in the moment.

Manifold insight, indeed.

Yet eight years prior to his farewell address, Eisenhower made a fateful decision that set our country and the world on a course from which we must find our way back.

The Road Not Taken

As background: In 1951, President Harry S Truman created a blue-ribbon commission to evaluate and propose a plan for the US energy future. The 1952 Paley Commission Report, named for the commission chair William S. Paley, proposed that the US build the economy on solar energy sources. The report also offered a strong negative assessment of nuclear energy and called for "aggressive research in the whole field of solar energy" as well as research and development on wind. In 1953, the new President Eisenhower ignored the report recommendation and inaugurated Atoms for Peace, touting nuclear power as the world's new energy miracle that would be "too cheap to meter," according to Lewis Strauss, chair of the US Atomic Energy Commission. Fundamentalist faith in nuclear energy abounded.

In that same period, photovoltaic, PV, solar cells were developed by Bell Laboratories for the new space program and used to power the Vanguard satellite. Our country was poised to make energy breakthroughs in PV, but, with the magic, millennialist bullet of nuclear power, photovoltaics were consigned to provide power for miniscule cells in watches and calculators. The revolution in solar-derived energy, which should have joined the personal computer revolution and the Internet, was aborted. When it revived much later, it did so elsewhere:—in Denmark, Germany, and Japan, where it yielded green jobs, industry, technical expertise, infrastructure, and market niche for renewable energy technologies.

Why the early myopia in energy policy? Scientists of the 1950s were seduced by the omnipotence of atomic fission and fusion, writes energy policy expert Hermann Scheer and author of the groundbreaking book, *Energy Autonomy*. An "arrogant fossil/nuclear worldview emerged," Scheer writes, that dismissed solar energy as backward and pre-industrial, as an "ideological fixation and technological pipedream"—precisely, Scheer posits, what the proponents of nuclear power themselves were guilty of.

How Clean Is Clean?

Today, despite decades of mega investments in and substantial subsidies for nuclear energy as estimated from 1950 to 2007 compared to those for renewable technologies as estimated from the 1970s to 2007, solar-derived technologies have outpaced nuclear power in rate of growth, cost-effectiveness, and job creation. Even so, given the growing specter of climate change, policy talk about a "nuclear renaissance" abounds nationally and internationally. Nuclear power is touted as a zero-carbon energy source and then bundled in with renewable energy technologies as the mix of clean energy technologies we must pursue to eliminate climate-change-driving CO_2 emissions. With nuclear in the mix, one wonders "How clean is clean?"

The adverse environmental health, international security, and economic impacts of nuclear power far outweigh its energy benefits. In its full life cycle, nuclear power:

- generates radioactive tailings at mine and mill sites, which endanger indigenous communities
- generates the suspected carcinogen and mutagen DU used in weapons and warfare, and
- creates long-lived and highly radioactive spent nuclear fuel with no disposal solution for future generations to cope with

Nuclear power plants routinely release small amounts of radioactive isotopes during operation, and they can release large amounts during accidents. For that reason, a 2003 expert panel of the National Academy of Sciences recommended that potassium iodide pills be provided to everyone forty and younger who lives near a nuclear power plant to protect against exposure to radioactive iodine.

In this era of unconventional war, nuclear power plants are vulnerable to sabotage and attack. Existing evacuation plans in case of an accident at a nuclear power plant are widely regarded as unrealistic paper exercises.

Energy reliance on water-intensive technologies, such as nuclear power, is an ill-fated relationship, as illustrated in the summer 2003 heat wave that gripped half of Europe and caused a record number of deaths. The prolonged heat wave triggered a water shortage resulting in insufficient water for electricity production for air conditioning. Hydropower production declined, and nuclear power plants shut down, causing industrial activity shutdowns, computer crashes, and harvest failures.

Finally and ominously, nuclear power reactors generate the fissile materials enriched to fuel nuclear bombs and inevitably create the risk of nuclear weapons development. Thus, atoms for peace are ineluctably atoms for war and terrorism. Else, why would Interpol, Europol, and other international organizations have initiatives to counter nuclear terrorism? As the UNESCO study on the Ethics of Nuclear Energy Technology states, "nuclear energy-using countries, which enrich their own uranium are nearly *de facto* nuclear weapons possessing states."

Carbon-Free, Nuclear-Free Future

How can we achieve a carbon-free, nuclear-free future? For one, the US can emulate the commitment to conservation, mandatory green building design, renewable energy technologies, and fuel-efficient practices in Europe, which reduced the average carbon use per capita to one-half that of the average American by 2011. In that same year Europe had three times the wind power of the US, and photovoltaic capacity was growing by seventy percent annually. Renewables fueled forty percent of Sweden's energy needs and fourteen percent of Germany's electricity compared to six percent of US electricity.

Recycled energy from cogeneration—combined heat and power—systems constituted from twenty to fifty percent of energy use in many European countries compared to eight percent in the US, according to 2011 data and policy. The fuel standard set for European vehicles was fifty miles per gallon by 2012 compared to the US average of thirty-five and one-half mpg by 2016. The EU earmarked more than three times the amount of money for high-speed trains than did the Obama administration. Were the United States to achieve the fuel economy standards of Europe, demand for oil would drop by an estimated twenty percent-an urgent thought, given the 2010 oil pollution tragedy in the Gulf of Mexico and climate crisis.

A critically acclaimed 2007 study, *Carbon-Free and Nuclear-Free: A Roadmap for US Energy Policy* prepared by the Nuclear Policy Research Institute and the Institute for Energy and Environmental Research, lays out a carbon-free and nuclear-free roadmap for US energy policy. The study analyzed more than twenty-five then available and nearly available renewable technologies, green building design, high efficiency vehicles and fuels for readiness for large-scale use, next steps for large-scale implementation, and CO2 abatement costs. The overarching finding is that "a zero-CO2 energy economy could be achieved within the next thirty to fifty years without the use of nuclear power." Further, the 2007 study found that eliminating CO_2 emissions could be achieved with "available or foreseeable technologies," at affordable cost, without buying carbon credits from other countries, and with phasing out oil imports within twenty-five years, by 2032.

Historically, renewable energy systems have not been given market and public policy parity with nuclear power. Even without market equity, solar-derived renewables in 2011 provided the same percent energy as nuclear power in the United States and were on an industrial growth curve with prices rapidly dropping while those of the decades-old nuclear industry only escalated. No new nuclear plant had come on line in the United States since 1974. Consider the 2009 statement by Jon Wellinghoff, then chairman of the Federal Energy Regulatory Commission, that new coal and nuclear plants were unnecessary and a poor choice of energy investment compared to renewables.

We Americans need a revolution in carbon-free, nuclear-free conservation, efficiency, and renewable technology scenarios to assure they are developed and implemented for local control with democratic values and freed from multinational control and militaristic dual uses. As the largest overconsumer of the world's finite resources and the instigator of nuclear power, we owe the world that moral debt.

Obama at the Crossroads

By 2011, the Obama administration lingered at a crossroads, taking the politically safe, pseudo-scientific position that our energy future is a mix of "clean" nuclear and renewable energy technologies. *It should have been time for the Obama Administration and Congress to take the road not taken in 1953 by:*

+ updating and expanding the wise, feasible recommendations of the Paley Commission, and
+ giving renewable energy systems market priority using all the mechanisms of public policy: investment in research and development, tax credits, green job training, technical assistance to businesses, standards for new building and renovations, and public sector conversion of buildings and vehicles to renewables

Passive Solar House

In 1980, I designed a passive solar house based on my environmental engineering master's thesis. Our builder was eager to learn solar design and went on to build dozens of similar houses over the next year in Franklin and Hampshire counties.

Federal and state tax credits for solar heating stimulated local industry and jobs, including small building businesses, a rooftop solar hot water heater build/install industry, and other related businesses. By the end of 1981, Ronald Reagan had removed the solar hot-water panels from the White House roof and eliminated solar tax credits. Demand for solar house design declined. New niche solar companies closed up shop, research and development funding for renewables—*the largest effort in the world between 1974 and 1981*-dried up.

Reliance on fossil fuels and nuclear energy was reinstated as the direction of US energy policy. Lesson learned: together with social demand through political activism and green business initiatives, federal and state policy is a determining factor in sustainable energy and our climate future,

Originally published February 3, 2011 at *Science for Peace*. Reprinted with permission.

Chernobyl's Tragedy-Induced Lessons

In 2011, Mikhail Gorbachev, last leader of the Soviet Union, published *Chernobyl Twenty-Five Years Later: Many Lessons Learned.*

In his retrospective, he cited three foremost lessons:

- ✦ needed public oversight of the secretive and deceptive nuclear industry
- ✦ the new threat of terrorism to nuclear plants, and
- ✦ the urgency of building a secure energy future, from solar, wind, and water

His statement could be construed as an aging statesman's apologia for his role in the Soviet Union's secrecy and slow response to the Chernobyl, Ukraine, nuclear meltdown, the world's worst industrial accident prior to Fukushima. After all, it was Sweden who alerted the world to radioactive fallout from the Chernobyl nuclear plant explosion, not the Soviet Union, and Gorbachev endangered residents by delaying evacuation.

Seventy tons of combusted nuclear fuel and seven hundred tons of radioactive graphite blanketed the disaster site. Belarus, western Russia, and rich farmland of the Ukraine were severely contaminated. Fearful of acute food shortages, Soviet authorities relaxed permissible levels of radioactivity in agricultural land. Winds carried fifty tons of fine particles to many parts of Europe and throughout the Northern Hemisphere, blanketing seventy-seven thousand square miles with radioisotopes of iodine, cesium, strontium, and plutonium. As a result, hunting, fishing, and foraging remained restricted in many contaminated regions of mainland Europe and the British Isles.

The cost of Chernobyl—in death and illness as well as social cynicism and anomie—is incalculable. Distrust of Soviet authorities grew so rapidly following the accident that many affected people refused to take protective potassium iodide pills belatedly distributed by the government. In 2006, the Ukrainian health minister reported that more than 2.4 million Ukrainians suffered health effects from the Chernobyl catastrophe. The highest estimate of overall mortality from the Chernobyl explosion and fire during the period from April 1986 to the end of 2004 is 985,000 people. And some analysts attribute the collapse of the Soviet Union beginning in 1989 to the "psychic blow" of Chernobyl: nuclear power had the status of a "sacred cow," its cadre of engineers and administrators, a sacred caste, according to Stephanie Cooke in her 2009 book, *In Mortal Hands*, an account of the nuclear age.

Gorbachev did not mince words, calling Chernobyl a "tragedy . . . beyond comprehension" and "a shocking reminder of the reality of the nuclear threat." Unbeknownst to most people, he wrote, there have been "some 150 significant radiation leaks at nuclear power stations over the world." He now works to implement his tragedy-induced lessons. As founding president of Green Cross International with branches in thirty-one countries, he has headed the international Climate Change Task Force to help ensure a just, sustainable, and secure future.

Like Gorbachev, the ex prime minister of Japan Naoto Kan, who resigned in the wake of disastrous management of the Fukushima nuclear emergency, became a critic of nuclear power and an apostle of renewable technologies. Government and industry secrecy about the extremity of the Fukushima crisis, mismanagement and crisis, and false pride in Japan's technological prowess that perpetuated a myth of nuclear safety—all risked destroying his country, said Nan. With other Japanese lawmakers, he launched a group "to create a roadmap for ending the country's reliance on nuclear power."

Chernobyl and Fukushima abound with morbid lessons–about unmanageable nuclear accidents, myths of nuclear safety, human and environmental costs far exceeding energy benefits, and blinding technological hubris. Some countries heeded them and abandoned nuclear power, among them Germany, Japan, Italy, Spain, Belgium, and Switzerland. Others have not. By 2012, the US re-licensed more than seventy aging nuclear plants and still supports new plants as if we have some God-given immunity to human and technical accidents and uncertainties. The industry's grip on government persists despite the unequivocal admission by John Rowe, retired CEO of Exelon–a nuclear heavyweight and strong contributor to Obama–that nuclear power is not economically viable. If, as some allege, the US is destined by our cultural history of muscular technical prowess and frontier mentality in space and elsewhere, then why not direct our vaunted technical pragmatism to aggressively building secure and affordable renewable energy systems?

Carbon-free, Nuclear-free Future

Researchers Mark Z. Jacobson, Stanford University professor of civil and environmental engineering and director of its Atmosphere/ Energy Program, and Mark A. Delucchi, research scientist at

University of California Berkley and Davis and Lawrence Berkeley National Laboratory have laid out a roadmap for energy policy in the next two to four decades by using a mix of energy efficiency, wind, water, and solar technologies. The barriers to achieving a renewable national and global energy system, according to the authors of "A Pathway to Sustainable Energy by 2030" in the *Scientific American*, are fundamentally political and social, not technological or economic. Security analyst Michael Klare, Hampshire College professor of peace and world security studies, wrote in 2012 that we were at a crossroads—one to cannibalize environmental legislation and "gain access to additional stores of difficult-to-get oil and gas on coastal and wilderness areas" and the other, intense and substantial investment in renewable energies.

And in our corner of the world-the evacuation zone of the decommissioned Vermont Yankee nuclear power plant with its stored nuclear waste—we are locked in a democracy-driven power struggle, namely the people and State of Vermont vs. Entergy, [the plant's owner, that eventually shut down Vermont Yankee.]

From an energy standpoint, we are perilously near two tipping points. One is climate change largely caused by fossil fuels: some experts estimate we have no more than ten years before irreversible effects ensue. The other is nuclear power; *a Fukushima-like accident in the US is only a matter of time*, according to nuclear expert Arnie Gundersen of Fairewinds.org. Precious little time remains. Needed bylaws and siting guidelines should be set so that wind and solar farms can be built with no more nuclear power plants constructed.

Originally published April 19, 2012 at *Portside*. Reprinted with permission.

Fukushima Five Years Later: Unfolding and Uncontrolled
co-written with Doug Renick

The media moved on some time ago from Fukushima and left most of us in the dark about that unfolding nuclear tragedy. Such selective amnesia suited Japanese Prime Minister Shinzo Abe, who reported that all's well with the Fukushima cleanup and the gradual return of resident refugees, as he looked forward to the anticipated 2020 summer Olympics in Tokyo.

Not so, reported others. In December 2015, Naohiro Masuda, Fukushima decommission chief, warned that the cleanup of the most complex industrial accident in history is far from solved. "Nothing can be promised," Masuda said, "not even robots have been able to enter the main fuel-debris areas so far. This is something that has never been experienced. A textbook doesn't exist for something like this. New science will have to be invented for the plant to be cleaned."

To keep that paramount industrial accident from slipping into the dim past, let us examine the ongoing history of the Fukushima tragedy. Five years ago on March 11, 2011, the Great East Japan Earthquake and ensuing tsunami devastated northeast Japan, killing and injuring more than twenty thousand people and crippling the Fukushima Dai'ichi nuclear power plant. Three of the plant's six reactors suffered hazardous nuclear core meltdowns and hydrogen gas explosions, releasing radionuclides into the air, soil, and Pacific Ocean.

More than 160,000 people were eventually evacuated from the region, and most remain today nuclear refugees living with the same trauma, fear, sense of displacement, and loss of livelihood and social roots as war refugees. So difficult has been their fate that, by late 2015, thirty-two hundred refugees had died of insufficient medical services, exhaustion of relocating, suicide, or, likely, heartbreak. In a callous move to keep schools open in Fukushima, the Japanese government raised the "permissible" level of radiation for children. Japanese children could be exposed to twenty-times more radiation per year than previously allowed, a level comparable to the yearly limit for radiation workers.

Just one year after the Fukushima emergency, the Japanese government claimed the area had been cleaned and encouraged farmers from Fukushima Prefecture to return to their agricultural fields. Little more than a year later, the farmers confronted the government in a public forum once they had learned that the government was allowing the sale of their produce despite finding it contaminated with radioactive cesium. One irate farmer dared the officials to feed cesium-contaminated produce to their children. Another conscience-stricken farmer lamented, "Customers think it's clean, but I would not dare eat this produce myself. We farmers feel guilty about selling it to others. There is no longer joy in farming."

For the past five years, radioactive water from the Fukushima site has poured via groundwater into the Pacific Ocean at the rate of three hundred tons per day, the largest accidental release of radioactive contaminants to the oceans in history. Radioactive cesium, a carcinogen that accumulates in animal, fish, and human tissue, has been found throughout mainland Japan including hotspots affecting living things in Tokyo; in fish off the coast of Fukushima, thus closing that industry; and in large migratory fish such as Bluefin tuna off the coast of California.

To stanch the flow of millions of gallons of groundwater from the immensely hazardous reactors into the ocean, the owner, TEPCO, has constructed a frozen underground wall around the radioactive reactor buildings to divert groundwater around them, a diversion they claim will reduce the contaminated groundwater to one-tenth its current volume.

However, technological optimism is increasingly foiled by the unexpected. In September 2015, ocean surges from Typhoon Etau overwhelmed the site's drainage pumps and hundreds of tons of radioactive water leaked from the reactors site and ultimately to the ocean. What, then, of more severe-typhoons, undersea earthquakes, and the reality of sea-level rise estimated at anywhere from three to fifteen feet within fifty years for the oceanside plant? How will an underground sea wall and onsite drainage systems survive natural disasters worsened by climate change?

Dissident Views

In a December 15, 2015 interview, Mitsuhei Murata, former Japanese ambassador to Switzerland, acknowledged, "It's common knowledge Fukushima is not at all under control. In Fukushima, he said, the government has allowed residents to come back at an exposure limit four times that of Chernobyl.

"This is a most serious humanitarian matter, if we think about the health of children," he stated. "So I am asserting the evacuation of children is urgently needed." He concluded that Japan must seek an honorable retreat from hosting the 2020 Olympics.

Echoing his concerns, former Prime Minister Yukio Hatoyama acknowledges that, while the government has claimed the Fukushima decommissioning and cleanup is proceeding well in order to hold the 2020 Olympic Games, it is a grave and uncontrolled situation.

Former Prime Minister Kan, under whose term the nuclear disaster occurred, concurs. "The accident is still unfolding," he told the National Press Club in Washington.

Voices from Fukushima, a reader's play was performed on March 13, 2016 in First Churches Lyman Hall in Northampton to commemorate the fifth anniversary of the nuclear power tragedy at Fukushima Daiichi in northeast Japan. The play invites you to imagine yourself in a voluntary evacuation zone, like the residents in Fukushima, to listen to the voices of the people whose lives are directly affected by nuclear energy and to discover a connection between your lifestyle and their livelihood.

Pat Hynes and Doug Renick are members of Nuclear- and Carbon-Free Future Coalition of Western Massachusetts, which sponsored dramatic readings in surrounding communities of *Voices from Fukushima.*

Originally published March 9, 2016 in the *Greenfield Recorder*. Reprinted with permission.

Fukushima Ten Years Later

There is a shortage of Fukushima health studies; there are big earthquake aftershocks rattling reactors and waste tanks, corporate and government dishonesty about decontamination, novel radioactive particles recently dispersed, and renewed fish contamination, writes John La Forge, editor of *Nukewatch* in the spring 2021 issue.

Only thyroid cancer has been studied in some depth, showing a significant increase in children exposed. Six major earthquake aftershocks from the 2011 earthquake in the Fukushima area have taken place. One swept away an unknown number of bags storing radioactive debris stacked near a river. Fukushima residents are fighting the state plan to use radiation-contaminated soil on roads. There are no remediation plans for the majority of forested areas within the extensive contamination zone. Highly contaminated treated wastewater stored in tanks is still heavily contaminated despite treatment. The government of Japan has given the nuclear plant owner TEPCO permission to discharge the treated wastewater into the Pacific Ocean, beginning in 2023, to the fury of nearby China and South Korea.

Recent releases of large cesium-contaminated particles have been detected on surface soils in the vicinity of the destroyed reactors. Recent critical reports state that the large contaminated area around the site is not safe for residents and that the 30-40 year timeline for decommissioning the site plant is unrealistic.

Climate Change and Nuclear Power: Magnifying the Risks

The *World Nuclear Industry Status Report 2012* portrays an industry reeling and in decline from the multiple impacts of world recession, the Fukushima tragedy, and immense competition from renewable energy development and natural gas. Nineteen reactors shut down in 2011 while only seven came on line. Four industrial countries announced phaseouts of their nuclear power plants: Germany, Belgium, Switzerland, and Taiwan. At least five countries that planned for nuclear power have declined to do so: Egypt, Italy, Jordan, Kuwait and Thailand. China and others have delayed new construction starts. This is a partial portrait of the industry in free fall.

Likewise, the US industry is walking away from nuclear power. John Rowe, former board chair and CEO of Exelon, America's largest producer of nuclear power with twenty-two nuclear power plants, said in March 2012 that nuclear power is not economically feasible. "I've never met a nuclear plant I didn't like, but it just isn't economic," Rowe said. Even so, both major US political parties and presidential candidates continue to enable the failed industry even as wind and solar have outpaced it in growth, economics, and citizen support.

Compounding the devil's bargain our government has struck with nuclear power is a set of climate-change factors that heighten its risks to ecosystems and human health and erode the technological hubris that keeps the industry afloat. Nuclear power was designed with the climate scenarios of the 1950s and 1960s, pre-dating the climate change epoch we are in. It is rapidly being challenged by extremes of weather in five inter-related ways:

+ dependence on massive amounts of water vs. extended periods of drought

- growing production losses and shutdowns from record-breaking heat and drought with consequent reliance on fossil fuels to fill the production gap
- shutdowns of nuclear power plants due to extreme flooding
- overheated cooling water causing severe thermal pollution of aquatic ecosystems, and
- threat of drought-induced wildfires spreading radioactive contamination

Heat and Drought

The most severe impact of heat and drought on nuclear power occurred in summer 2003 when the worst heat wave since 1540 gripped half of Europe and killed thousands of people, primarily elderly. Hydro production lessened, and seventeen nuclear reactors in France reduced their power output or shut down. Related impacts included industrial shutdown, computer systems crashing, harvest failures, and excessive cost for replacement energy.

In mid August 2012 the Millstone Nuclear Power Station in Waterford, Connecticut, shut down one of its two reactors because seawater was too warm to cool it, something that its designers could not have conceived. For the first time in the reactor's history of thirty-seven years of operation, water withdrawn from Long Island Sound was too warm to use.

As of July 22, 2012, Illinois had issued a record twenty-nine exemptions to nuclear and coal-fired plants to discharge overheated so-called cooling water into rivers and lakes in order to provide peak demand electricity. State law sets the threshold for discharge water at ninety degrees Fahrenheit, but the limit allowed under emergency variance has reached nearly one hundred degrees.

"This has been a problem for years, and it's only getting worse," according to River Network, whose mission is to protect the nation's freshwater resources. Wendy Wilson, director of rivers, energy, and climate for River Network, said of the trend, "We have terrible thermal pollution problems in this country, and the result is dead and dying rivers."

Flooding

The Fort Calhoun, Nebraska, nuclear power plant was shut down in April 2011 through December 2013 due to the plant being partially submerged by extreme flooding from the Missouri River and unresolved safety violations, including deficiencies on flood planning. As for the integrity of the soil underneath the facility, nothing was determined early on regarding its load-bearing soundness. Nor was there any immediate study of on-site contaminated soil carried downstream with the floods.

Wildfires

In August 2010, wildfires caused by record-breaking drought and heat wave consumed huge swaths of western Russia and choked Moscow and other large cities with air pollution. The Russian emergency minister warned that fire-induced winds could carry radioactive particles hundreds of miles from the burning trees, plants, and forest soil around Chernobyl, reaching cities in Russia and beyond. Given the thirty-year half-lives of strontium-90 and cesium-137 released from Chernobyl, they will take three hundred years to fully decay and thus remain hazardous for the growing occurrences of climate-change induced droughts and fires.

Additional Climate-Related Threats

The US Nuclear Regulatory Commission has concealed the risk of upstream dam failures capable of causing meltdowns of nuclear plant reactors, as revealed by an NRC whistleblower. Thirty-four nuclear reactors are sited downstream from dams. In 2012, Superstorm Sandy slowed or shut down a half dozen US nuclear power plants, and the nation's oldest facility at Oyster Creek, New Jersey, confirmed a rare alert after record storm surge endangered a vital cooling system for the spent fuel rods.

Nuclear power is neither clean nor reliable as 2012 presidential candidates Barack Obama and Mitt Romney avowed that it is. Nor is it an answer to climate change, as some scientists and activists have asserted. It is, rather, a *wolf in zero-carbon clothing* whose adverse public health, international security, and economic and climate-change risks outweigh any touted benefits.

Originally published Winter, 2012 in *Nukewatch Quarterly*. Reprinted with permission.

Pursuing Equality for All Women

Women belong in all places where decisions are being made.

—Ruth Bader Ginsburg

Who among us has not had singular moments that shaped the path of our lives? The following articles flow from certain defining moments in my life and my consciousness. The themes move from local to international and, most important for me, join feminism inseparably with peace and social, racial, and environmental justice.

I became a committed feminist in the early 1970s when our society was pulsating with a revolution in women's rights and quest for equality. It burst forth in a seismic wave of creativity from music, theater, poetry, and women's literature and women's studies programs to health and law clinics, shelters for battered women, feminist bookstores, counseling centers, credit unions, self-defense classes, and softball teams. Hampshire Street in Inman Square, Cambridge, Massachusetts, had it all. And on that street, across from a women's health center and down the street from the feminist bookstore New Words, two of us opened Bread and Roses, a women's restaurant and center of culture described in the first article. Recently, the Commission on the Status of Women of the City of Cambridge completed a feminist walking tour of Hampshire Street commemorating that singular epoch in women's history.

Another life-shaping experience was travel to developing countries with my partner, Janice Raymond, when she directed the Coalition Against Trafficking in Women. In the Philippines, particularly, I met young women survivors of sexual exploitation in brothels opened near US military bases, biracial children rejected by US military fathers, and also mothers with extremely handicapped children due to the immense impact of US military pollution on nearby drinking water and landfills. An agreement with the Philippine government left the US free of obligation to clean up US military base pollution. And so the US military left immense quantities of toxins in place that sickened Philippine civilians—pregnant women disproportionately—relocated to US military bases in the wake of Mount Pinatubo's huge volcanic eruption in 1991.

All that I witnessed and learned from interviews with victims and survivors I shared with my graduate students in classes at Boston University School of Public Health. A doctoral seminar on the health effects of war, for which I did in-depth reading and drew from my experience in the Philippines for my talk on the health effects of war on women, set the course of my path once I retired from BU.

In the eleven years since 2010 as director and subsequently board member of the Traprock Center for Peace and Justice, in western Massachusetts, I have never finished learning, writing, and speaking about the baleful harm of war and militarism especially to its victims, to its perpetrators, to our natural environment and the climate crisis, to national budget priorities, and to humanism and democracy. This chapter spotlights the benefits of women's equality not only for ourselves but also for our world, a reality I beheld while participating in the 2018 African Women's Feminist Peace Conference in Accra, Ghana, one of the most inspiring and instrumental experiences of my life.

The following thematic citations are drawn from writings included in the following articles.

> The degree of equality of women within countries predicts best–better than the degree of democracy; better than the level of wealth, income inequality or ethno-religious identity–how peaceful or conflict-ridden their countries are.
>
> —African Feminists: A Key to Global Peace

> Governments on all sides of war have initiated, accommodated, and tolerated military brothels under the aegis of "rest and recreation" for their soldiers, with the private admission that a regulated system of brothels will contain male sexual aggression,

limit sexually transmitted diseases in the military, and boost soldiers' morale for war.

—Ten Reasons Why Militarism is Bad for Women

Armed groups target children for their wars because children and more so girls . . ."are obedient, vulnerable, and malleable."

—Girl Soldiers: Forgotten Casualties of War

Blessed are the steadfast Mothers in Military Families Against the War who urge and exhort for an end to wars in Afghanistan and the occupation of Iraq, to bring their children home, and for the recognition of the exorbitant costs of these wars to our country.

—Mother's Day for Peace: A Blessing

With support from family, community, and nation, and the full realization of her rights, a ten-year-old girl can thrive and help bring about the future we all want. What the world will look like in fifteen years will depend on our doing everything in our power to ignite the potential of the ten-year-old girl today.

—Female Equality Is Key to a Sustainable Future

"Like white people challenging whiteness, it is men who must do the work of understanding that a significant portion of our identity is based on a toxic, patriarchal masculinity."
—The Independent Woman: Extracts from The Second Sex

Bread and Roses Restaurant
The Women's Restaurant Inc. 1974-1978

In December 1974, Bread and Roses opened its doors in Cambridge, Massachusetts, as a woman-owned business for women and their friends that included a gourmet vegetarian restaurant and center for feminist culture with weekly events and gatherings. The name Bread and Roses was adopted from the demand of the women-led textile strikers in Lowell, Massachusetts, in 1912: "We want bread and roses, too."

Bread and Roses was co-founded by Pat Hynes and Gill Gane and opened following five months of renovating a dank, dismal neighborhood bar. With the exception of plumbing, all the renovation was done by women—architectural design, electrical work, carpentry, sheet-rocking, plastering, and painting—all accompanied by high-volume songs of the new feminist and lesbian music albums.

We launched Bread and Roses by selling a hundred shares of stock for a hundred dollars a share to women investors. In lieu of tips, Bread and Roses paid above minimum wage and, through donations, supported a feminist cause each week, including Rosie's Place, Boston, for poor and homeless women and other new feminist projects and businesses opening in the zeitgeist of the 1970s women's movement. Every Sunday evening, we provided our leftover meals to the local shelter—the first in Cambridge—for women victims of domestic violence.

As for feminist cultural events, individual women artists exhibited their fine and applied artwork every two weeks. Many had never shown their art publicly and told stories of bringing their artwork out of the seclusion of their attics to the restaurant exhibit space. Radical feminist writers and speakers, including Andrea Dworkin and Mary Daly, novelists such as Tillie Olsen and Alice Walker, and dozens of others including activists, athletes, and scientists spoke at our Sunday evening events. Among the highlights of those years were the vibrant concerts of young feminist and lesbian musicians, among them Alix Dobkin and Willie Tyson, who electrified weekend evenings with their woman-identified music and wit.

As for other memorable evenings, there was the night a woman rushed into Bread and Roses, almost breathless, saying, "I just arrived from Ireland, and this is the first place I wanted to visit." (Before the age of the Internet, how did she know?) Another evening, Margaret Mead walked in with her daughter Mary Catherine Bateson. Mead, small, clothed in a floor-length tunic, and holding a walking stick twice her height, peered at the all-woman staff in the open kitchen and the feminist posters lining the walls, as she might have done coming onto a new culture or race of people. We suspected she might be working on a new study of the tsunami of second-wave feminism sweeping through Inman Square down Hampshire Street!

We sold Bread and Roses to young feminists who opened in 1978 as Amaranth Restaurant. In turn, Amaranth sold to Daddio's

Restaurant, to which name a Cambridge city councilwoman replied, "Given its history, do you have to name it Daddio's?" Today, a well-loved woman-owned restaurant, Oleana, occupies 137 Hampshire Street, the address of the former Bread and Roses.

Bread is life's prose

Poetry, the rose.

Bread and Roses

the women's restaurant, cultural center, and softball team
1974-1978

a real (i)deal

velveted steel

Poem originally published in *On the River, Cambridge Community Poem*, Peter Payack. editor.

African Feminists: A Key to Global Peace

The days when one could claim that the situation of women
had nothing to do with matters of
national and international security are, frankly, over . . .
—Valerie M. Hudson

On the eve of World War II, the iconic British writer Virginia Woolf responded to a male attorney's question about how to prevent war. To prevent war, she replied, women must be educated and able to earn a living. Only then, not dependent on fathers and brothers, can women possess "disinterested influence" to exert against war. Your question, she continued, is "how to prevent war." Ours is, "Why fight?"

Peace and the security of nations are powerfully linked with the equality of women, though it is the rare power broker–be they diplomat or military liaison–who acknowledges it.

I traveled to Ghana in 2018 to participate in the International Feminist Peace Congress organized by the Women's International League for Peace and Freedom, WILPF. My interviews—with western women prior to the Congress and with African women and a few men during their sessions on feminist peace in Africa— reinforced the mounting conviction that *the fate of nations is tied to the status of women.*

WILPF members from the Democratic Republic of the Congo assemble.
photo copyright by Pat Hynes

WILPF members from the war-ridden Democratic Republic of the Congo, DRC, grasp the totality of that conviction. The congress pulsated throughout with vibrant color and bold geometric designs woven into African clothing, wall hangings, and tablecloths. Wearing traditional clothing with electrifying color and patterns emblazoned with the French words "rien sans les femmes," literally *nothing without women*, DRC members elaborated to me, "We mean everywhere throughout the world. If women are not involved, nothing of critical use to the world will happen."

While preparing for the conference, two dichotomous realities claimed my thoughts. The first: feminist revolutions to gain human rights and equality for women have—without weapons, without fists, without a drop of blood spilled—freed and saved the lives of millions of women and girls. The second: hundreds of millions of women have been injured, harmed, and killed by patriarchal institutions and by misogynist men. Why? Because they are women. How? With weapons and rape in war, with fists and rape at home, through the commercial sex trade, and through the *slow gendered violences* of personal and public inequality.

Peace is quintessentially a women's issue, most clearly when the continuum of male violence against women in its private, social, and structural dimensions is grasped. "That continuum of violence," British feminist and author Cynthia Cockburn relayed to me by email, "persists along a scale of force (fist to nuclear bomb), space (the home, the street, the village, the city, the battlefield, and the nation), and time (pre-war, wartime, and postwar)."

"Here's where gender comes in," she continued. "There is no escaping the tendency of men and masculinity in most if not all cultures to feature as actors in violence, women as acted upon. And you can't expect a government that promotes and pays for the shaping of men as war fighters, often condoning rape as a weapon of war, to foster a civil culture in which male violence against women is noticed, deplored, and punished as it should be."

Recent, groundbreaking analysis validates those convictions.

A team of researchers, including security studies experts and statisticians, has created the largest global database on the status of women, WomanStats, and compared the security and level of conflict within 175 countries to the overall security of women in those countries. Their findings are profoundly illuminating for global security and world peace. The degree of equality of women within countries predicts best–better than degree of democracy and better than level of wealth, income inequality, or ethno-religious identity—how peaceful or conflict-ridden their countries are. Further, democracies with higher levels of violence against women are less stable and are more likely to choose force rather than diplomacy to resolve conflict.

Violence against women is an invisible foundation underlying local, national, and international politics and security. It "has a causal impact on intrastate and interstate conflict," Womanstats researcher Dr. Mary Caprioli told me. Her colleague Dr. Valerie Hudson prospectively reframed their central study finding: "Increasing gender equality is expected to have cascading effects on security, stability, and resilience" within a country and internationally.

What are universal indicators that manifest equality and inequality of women in a country, as compiled in WomanStats? On a personal level, they comprise the multifarious forms of violence against women, including:

+ sexual violence, sex trafficking, and prostitution
+ genital mutilation
+ sex-selective abortion, female infanticide, and neglect of girls because of preference for sons, and
+ preventable maternal mortality

Consider the following staggering finding calculated by the creators of the comprehensive database: *More lives were lost in the twentieth century through violence against women in all its forms than during all twentieth-century wars and civil strife.* Yet, while thousands of monuments throughout the United States honor those who gave their lives for their country in war, only one—the first of its kind—is being planned for women who lost their lives giving birth to the country's children.

Personal and family-status law further adds to women's and girls' inequality and mortality when women cannot divorce, are impoverished by divorce, or stay in stultifying and violent relationships to avoid destitution. When girls are forced into child marriage, they face the grave risk of complications from pregnancy and childbirth, the major cause of death globally for teenage girls aged fifteen to nineteen.

Inheritance and property laws that deprive women of resources comparable to those inherited by their brothers and husbands ultimately impoverish women, a form of economic violence. Because women's reproduction and care for children and extended family are not compensated, women are cheated of savings, pension, and Social Security. Consequently, *the greatest risk factor for being poor in old age is having been a mother*, according to WomanStats researchers.

Rampant discriminatory workplace policies that deny women equal pay for equal work and merited promotions are workplace and societal forms of economic violence against women. Worse for working mothers in many countries is the persistent "motherhood penalty"–whereby they are further set back financially by lack of paid parental leave and government-funded child care.

At the structural level of governance, the glaring absence of women in national government as well as international bodies such as the UN at every echelon, particularly the highest, robs women of power and, consequently, the world of security. In 2018, at the time of the African Women's Feminist Peace Conference, only twenty women held the office head of state or head of government, a mere 6.3 percent versus 93.7 percent male international leaders.

Ironically, the United States—touting itself as a beacon of democracy—required a quota of twenty-five percent women in legislatures of countries where it has waged war, Afghanistan and Iraq. Yet the US languished at just twenty percent in its own Congress in 2018, and, despite its narcissistic identity as "exceptional" and "necessary" for the world, the US has never elected a woman president.

No doubt the paucity of women in US governance is correlated with the rate of maternal mortality–the highest among industrial countries; with rampant sexual harassment exposed by the Me Too Movement; and with a dismal rating on the 2018 Global Peace index–121 out of 163 countries ranked.

What difference do women bring to issues of power and national security? Nearly two hundred women in politics surveyed in sixty-five countries agreed, "Women's presence in politics increases the amount of attention given to social welfare, legal protection, and transparency in government and business." Four-fifths of them expressed that women in government restore citizens' trust in government.

Evelyn Murphy, former Massachusetts lieutenant governor and secretary of environment, concurs. "Women typically run for public office and accept high, appointed government positions because they see problems they want to fix," she told me. "The women with whom

I worked brought to public governance their experiences in their families and the community institutions that support their families. That experience is deeply rooted in inclusivity. They exercise their power *with* others rather than *over* others."

Dr. Murphy cited recent advances in Massachusetts's public policy for gender equity in salary and paid family and medical leave. "They were propelled by women in government," she said. "Men were involved. But women were the driving force."

Studies of women in leadership in public and private sectors have concluded that women in high-level positions and on boards deal more effectively with risk, focus more strategically on long-term priorities, and are more successful financially. Experimental studies of women and men negotiating post-conflict agreements have found that all male groups take riskier, less empathic, and more aggressive positions. They also break down more quickly than negotiations that include women. Further, men are more satisfied with decisions made with women involved than those made with all-male groups.

Given that, *why aren't women equally represented at every peace negotiation*, as UN Security Council Resolution 1325 calls for, from those involving Afghanistan and Israel/Palestine to the Democratic Republic of the Congo?

Lawyer and mediator Ayo Ayoola-Amale, convener of the Ghana peace conference, underscored the critical potential and impact of women in peace negotiations.

The Liberian 2011 Nobel Prize laureate Leymah Gbowee, together with Christian and Muslim women, pressured warring parties into the 2003 negotiations that eventually ended years of horrific war in Liberia,

Ms. Ayoola-Amale told me.

Reinforcing Evelyn Murphy's experience in government, Ms. Ayoola-Amale elucidated,

Research has shown that where women's inclusion is prioritized, peace is more probable, especially when women are in a position to influence decision making. The reasons are not far-fetched. Women constantly bridge boundaries and build alliances for peace. They promote dialogue and build trust. Women take an inclusive approach whether it is stopping conflict, contributing to peace processes, or rebuilding their societies after conflict or war.

The director of WILPF Cameroon's communications and disarmament programs, Guy Blaise Feugap, explained to me the taproot of his commitment to feminist peace. "In my family, there was much domestic violence. Since I was young, I wanted to work against violence against women and on behalf of peace. Micro inequalities grow into macro inequalities, and I had the conviction that women are necessary for my country's development and the construction of peace. Women are excluded from high level decision-making, and I am committed to working for their inclusion." A teacher of Spanish and English, he has also written two novels with that core theme.

Nozizwe Madlala-Routledge, former member of parliament and assistant secretary of defense in the post-apartheid South African government, has turned the crucible of her experience into a lifelong commitment to equality for women in political decision-making. "The end of minority white rule," she told me, "did not end patriarchal, militarized rule. You enter office to change government, and government changes you. Being elected to office is not enough. Women and men of integrity must transform government."

That seasoned veteran of male-dominated politics laid out a strategic plan of action to the international conference audience. Components include:
- building the progressive feminist movement, particularly focusing on young women
- using our electoral power to elect gender-sensitive women and men of integrity
- working to "transform political parties so they promote women and feminist leadership, and
- demanding greater transparency in the financing of elections

The concept of "Rien sans les femmes"—nothing without women— infused her stirring opening speech.

Peacemaking within and among nations needs strategic and strong allies, yet nearly half the human race is overlooked. "Enough of paper talk"—protested many African women speakers exasperated by the exclusion of women from national peacekeeping and post-conflict resolution negotiations.

Having won gains for their equality and human rights without weaponizing their battles, peace-activist women have a history of strategic intelligence that governments and international bodies, such as the UN, urgently need, given ominous trends. Among them are:

+ the decline in peace since 2010 as measured by the Global Peace Index
+ the decline in democracy, with one-third of the world living in backsliding democracies
+ the stagnation of women and young people gaining high government positions, and
+ crushing capitalist trends in income inequality

Unless societies transform themselves with an analysis of the status of women's equality and act decisively to empower women, they will persist as repositories of male ambitions, male privilege, and male power. That toxic mix dooms the future of national and international security.

Our conference opened with a few minutes of silence to honor the great Ghanaian statesman, peacemaker, and former secretary general of the United Nations Kofi Annan, who died that morning. His words of many years ago embody the core message of the momentous African women's feminist peace conference:

> There is no policy more effective in promoting development, health, and education than the empowerment of women and girls and no policy is more important in preventing conflict or in achieving reconciliation after a conflict has ended.

In closing, traditional drumming and dancers drew everyone to their feet and into dance lines. "Arise women of Africa, women of the world," intoned one speaker. "Let a few hours here in Ghana resonate through Africa and the world."

Feminist peace-making in Africa is on the move.

Originally published September 25, 2018, at *Truthdig*. Reprinted with permission.

Ten Reasons Why Militarism is Bad for Women

We remained mired for years in the US war in Afghanistan and the US-led pre-emptive war against Iraq and occupation of the country that violated international law and the UN Charter. With one exception, none of the US administration protagonists have fought in a war. As one veteran wrote, "those who declare war should know [its price]." They should also know who pays the price. The greatest casualties of modern war are non-combatant civilians. Among civilian casualties, women and girls are deliberately targeted and grievously harmed by war. The following are ten reasons why militarism is bad for women.

1. Modern warfare kills massive numbers of women and childen.

Bombs and weapons kill and maim civilian women in numbers equal to civilian men killed and maimed during armed conflict. Throughout the twentieth century, a growing percentage of those killed in war were civilians. By the 1990s, nine of ten people who died in war from direct and indirect effects were civilians. The rise in the proportion of civilian deaths—and notably women's and children's deaths—in twentieth-century and twenty-first-century warfare is attributed to changes in war technology and war tactics, including urban warfare. High-tech war from the sky coupled with massive firepower has replaced army combat in the field, and military strategy employs so-called precision bombing to destroy civilian infrastructure such as power plants, water works, hospitals, industrial plants, and communications systems, as the US did in Iraq in 1991 and again in 2003.

2. Landmines injure and kill women.

Women and children are common casualties in agrarian and subsistence-farming societies where landmines intended to starve a people by killing its farmers have been deliberately placed in agricultural fields and along routes to water sources and markets. More than one hundred million antipersonnel landmines and unexploded ordnance lie dispersed and unmarked in fields, roadways, pasturelands, and near borders in ninety countries throughout the world. From fifteen- to twenty-thousand people are maimed or killed each year by those "weapons of mass destruction in slow motion," as landmines have been called, and more than seventy percent of reported victims are civilians.

Women constitute a larger percent of farmers than men in many parts of Asia and Africa and are responsible for up to eighty percent of food produced in many regions of Africa. When maimed by landmines, they lose the ability to farm and feed their families, and their husbands often abandon them, leaving them to beg on the streets or be sexually exploited.

3. Widows of war are displaced, disinherited, and impoverished.

The poorest widows, concludes the UN, are the old and frail, those with young children to shelter and feed, internally displaced and refugees, and those who have been widowed due to armed conflict.

In the war-torn countries of Angola, Bosnia-Herzegovina, Kosovo, Mozambique, and Somalia, the majority of adult women are widows. Seventy percent of Rwandan children were supported solely by mothers, grandmothers, or oldest girl children following the 1990s civil war there. Girls in Rwanda were heads of family for an estimated 58,500 households. In Kosovo, where an estimated ten thousand men died or disappeared, many widows who returned from refugee camps had no social safety nets and no advocacy organizations and became indigent and socially marginalized.

4. Women and children are the majority of war refugees.

Eighty percent of the world's refugees and internally displaced persons are women and children. The scale and nature of war in the late twentieth century resulted in unprecedented numbers of people fleeing conflict such that the displacement of people by war in the 1990s had more severe public health impact, in many situations, than the conflict itself.

In a refugee camp in Bangladesh, Burmese girls less than one year of age died at twice the rate of boys, and girls over five years of age and women died at 3.5 times the rate of males. Despite little gender-based data, many conclude that refugee women and girls have a higher mortality rate than men and boys because systems of health services and food provision in refugee camps privilege men and boys over women and girls.

5.   War fuels rape, sexual torture, and sexual exploitation.

A unique harm of war for women is the trauma inflicted when men wield women's bodies as weapons to demean, assault, and torture. Women were raped by knights and pilgrims in the Crusades; by soldiers in the American Revolutionary War; by Germans marching through Belgium in World War I and through Poland and Russia in World War II; by Russians as they took Berlin in World War II; by Pakistanis in the Bangladesh war of independence; by US soldiers during the occupation of Japan, in the Vietnam War, and in military bases in the Philippines and Korea; by Serbs and Rwandans for the intent of so-called ethnic cleansing; and by Indonesian pro-militia in retreat from East Timor as that country voted for independence. In a phrase, men on all sides of war harm women.

Military brothels, rape camps, and growing instances of sex trafficking for prostitution are fueled by the culture of war that relies on, licenses, and admires male aggression and by post-war social and economic ruin, which is particularly devastating for women and children. History reveals that senior officers of war and military occupation have sanctioned and normalized the sexual exploitation of local women by military men. Governments on all sides of war have initiated, accommodated, and tolerated military brothels under the aegis of "rest and recreation" for their soldiers with the private admission that a regulated system of brothels will contain male sexual aggression, limit sexually transmitted diseases in the military, and boost soldiers' morale for war.

6.   Aid workers and UN peacekeepers in post-conflict areas
     sexually exploit women and girls.

In February 2002, the United Nations High Commission for Refugees, UNHCR, and Save the Children released a report on their investigation into allegations of sexual abuse of West African refugee children in Guinea, Liberia, and Sierra Leone. Their interviews with fifteen hundred women, men, and child refugees revealed that girls between the ages of thirteen and eighteen were sexually exploited by male aid workers, many of whom were employed by national and international non-governmental organizations, NGOs, and the UN, and also by UN peacekeepers and community leaders.

An insidious outcome for women and girls in post-conflict areas is the epidemic of sexual exploitation aggravated by UN peacekeeping forces and international police. In Bosnia-Herzegovina, the trafficking of women and girls for prostitution grew exponentially after the Western protectorate was established at the end of the war in 1995. International police serving with the UN mission there facilitated the trafficking, accepted bribes from traffickers and brothel owners, purchased women and girls from traffickers, frequented brothels, and arranged for trafficked women and girls to be delivered to police residences.

7. Women and girls are at higher risk of STDs, including HIV infection, from soldiers and peacekeepers.

Rape and sexual exploitation by the military during war and in post-conflict situations has resulted in an epidemic of HIV infection, AIDS, and sexually transmitted diseases, STDs, among women and girls in war-torn countries. Rates of sexually-transmitted diseases are generally from two to five times higher in male military than in civilian populations and rise much higher during war, thus infecting those exploited during sexual encounters.

The first recorded cases of HIV among women in Cambodia occurred after peacekeepers were assigned to that country in 1992. Prior to their arrival, there was little prostitution. By 2002, an extensive sex industry existed in Cambodia, and the country had the highest prevalence of HIV infection in Asia.

8. Poor women and their children lose health, housing, education, and welfare services due to war-related pressures on services, and priorities of the military budget

Conflict diverts health resources away from health-care delivery and disease prevention to treating trauma. In Zenica, Bosnia, for example, the proportion of military and civilian surgical cases due to war-related trauma rose from twenty-two percent to seventy-eight percent in the city's major hospital during the first six months of the war in 1992, overwhelming medical services. In the same period, infant and child mortality nearly doubled, and newly diagnosed tuberculosis cases quadrupled.

Similarly, the US war against terrorism siphoned resources from social and health programs for the poorest of our country, single mothers and their children. As an example, the 2003 budget for biodefense was $5.9 billion, up more than three hundred percent from 2002, while forty-one million Americans lacked health insurance.

9. Women suffer higher rates of domestic violence from military husbands and partners.

The culture and training of violence spills over from the battlefield to the bedroom. Violence against women is endemic in military marriages. According to the Miles Foundation, military men are from two to five times as violent towards their wives as are other men. As an example, four women at Fort Bragg, North Carolina were brutally killed by their military officer husbands in the summer of 2002. Three of the murderers had recently returned from the war in Afghanistan.

10. Women are exposed to toxic chemical weapons and environmental contamination during and after war and from military activities.

By the end of the war in Vietnam, the United States had sprayed seventy-two million liters of chemicals on more than ten percent of Vietnam, an ecosystem of forests and wetlands. Two-thirds of the chemicals dispersed in the most massive use of chemical warfare in history were the dioxin-contaminated herbicide Agent Orange. An estimated 650,000 Vietnamese suffer from a mysterious complex of illnesses and chronic conditions. Five hundred thousand Vietnamese have died from conditions attributed to the chemical warfare exposure. Three to four generations of women have given birth to tens of thousands of deformed and disabled children.

Originally published in Spring 2003 at Issue 84 of the Population and Development Program *DifferentTakes series*, Hampshire College, Amherst, Massachusetts. Reprinted with permission.

Girl Soldiers: Forgotten Casualties of War

At the end of the reintegration queue for child soldiers
are girls, who are by and large invisible.

—Save the Children

Secretary of State Hillary Clinton was visibly shaken by information about sexual crimes against women and girls when she visited the Democratic Republic of Congo in 2009. Sexual crimes in that Central African country, known as the "rape capital of the world," included the sexual exploitation of tens of thousand of girls abducted and trapped as child soldiers. Nonetheless, President Barack Obama had waived a congressionally mandated ban on military aid to countries known to exploit child soldiers since 2010, among them the Democratic Republic of Congo, DRC.

The DRC's eastern region is exceedingly rich in rare earth minerals and exceedingly rife with decades of brutal war over those minerals. DRC and three other countries, Nigeria, Somalia, and South Sudan–each of which exploits thousands of child soldiers– were projected to receive more than $161 million in US military aid in FY 2016.

The US Child Soldiers Prevention Act of 2008 bans the US government from providing military resources and aid to countries that use soldiers younger than eighteen; however, it also allows a presidential waiver in cases of "national interest." But what possible "national interest" can override the lives of tens of thousands of children shattered in the worst of childhood nightmares–lives of being forced to torture, kill, rape, and, in the case of girls, lives of being serially raped and made pregnant?

The Reality

At any given time, some three hundred thousand children between the ages of eight and eighteen are exploited as child soldiers in scores of civil and international conflicts in Africa, Asia, and Colombia. In Sierra Leone's civil war, 1991-2001, eighty percent of fighters were between seven and fifteen years old. In Liberia's conflict, 1989-2003, up to seventy percent of government and rebel troops were children. Forty percent of soldiers slain in Colombia were children. The Lord's Resistance Army in Uganda has been mainly comprised of children.

Children who became soldiers in all of those wars were abducted from agricultural fields, while enroute to school or market, or when their village was attacked. Others joined for reasons of extreme poverty and hunger, fleeing family abuse, revenge for enemy brutality upon their family, drawn to a popular cause, and, in the case of some boys, respect from male elders. In-depth investigators of child soldiers conclude, "Never before in the history of warfare have children been so exploited on such a vast scale."

What most people do not realize is how large a percentage of child soldiers are girls–an estimated forty percent who are exploited like boy soldiers as servants, cooks, porters, spies, human shields, suicide bombers, and fighters. In Sri Lanka, more than forty percent of fifty thousand children in armed groups were girls, a finding determined during peace talks between warring parties and UNICEF. Deepening their trauma, girls are taken into sex slavery by boy soldiers, adult soldiers, and commanders. In some cases, girls are sold into sexual slavery for weapons. Given the popular image of boys as child soldiers, hundreds of thousands of girls constitute an invisible army and "forgotten casualties of war" in the rehabilitation process following cessation of armed conflict.

Armed groups target children for their wars because children—and *more so girls because of sex discrimination*—are "obedient, vulnerable, and malleable." Children can be more easily indoctrinated as the next generation of armed rebels and terrorists. Child soldiers are cheap because they are unpaid and eat less than adults. They provide functions such as cooking, cleaning, and portering, thus freeing up adult soldiers for more rigorous fighting. With the prevalence of light but deadly weapons, both girls and boys are trained for combat. In a 2002 survey, nearly half the interviewed girls in armed groups described their primary role as fighter.

Despite their utility as fighters and servants, girl soldiers are raped, prostituted, mutilated, infected with STDs including HIV/AIDS, and made pregnant by soldiers. Many are permanently injured and will suffer lifelong pain as a result of multiple rapes and untreated infections. Returning to their villages and homes, numerous girls have reported that they are rejected as filthy and immoral, and they are blamed for disgracing family and community honor. Even more punished are girls who return pregnant or with children born of rape. Losing family and social support, they are compelled to turn to prostitution or stay with an abusive ex-soldier "husband" to raise the child and survive. Moreover, even after commitments to release child soldiers, armed groups refuse to give up girls, holding them captive as "wives." Thus, the full cycle of misogyny entraps girls, ruthlessly violated as child soldiers, ostracized when returning home, and often not released in the so-called peace process.

Fifteen-year-old Grace Akallo was abducted in 1996 with twenty-nine other high school girls from her boarding school dormitory at St. Mary's college campus in northern Uganda by warlord Joseph Kony and rebel soldiers of the Lord's Resistance Army. The girls were pushed to the point of physical death, walking barefoot, given little food and water, and beaten with sticks and the butts of rifles. They were driven to the point of spiritual death, being forced to torture and kill other children—sometimes a sibling—in a seasoning process to dehumanize them, extinguish their consciences, and break their wills. Kony forced the girls to train with AK-47s and also distributed them among his commanders as "wives." Even with babies strapped to their backs, they were expected to fight.

Grace was given to a man "older than her father," who on first encounter seized her and raped her. "I felt like a thorn was in my skin as my innocence was destroyed," she wrote of his sexual violence. Further, the stigma of rape is so extreme in her community that ex-girl soldiers will admit to murder before they admit to having been raped.

In contrast to the outcast plight of girl soldiers, many boy soldiers earn a manly status in their communities. Leymah Gbowee, the Liberian Nobel Peace Prize laureate, worked with ex-child soldiers from Charles Taylor's army during Liberia's civil war. Joseph, whom she counseled, explained that he became a child soldier because "boys who joined the rebellion came back and were really respected and were often seen in the company of the elders and community leaders."

Gbowee is convinced that the nexus between violence, weapons, and manhood is responsible for drawing many former boy soldiers into the brutal, macho cycle of war. Many of the girls she assisted were "child wives" of the ex-soldiers and had been abducted, raped, and beaten into submission. With no exit, each girl was "caught up in a spiral of one individual trying to prove his maleness." The abuse women suffer during conflict, she observed, "is a reflection of the interaction between men and women, boys and girls, during peace time."

Compounding the excruciating burdens of girl soldiers is the failure for them of the UN and international NGO "disarmament, demobilization, and reintegration, DDR" programs intended to help former child soldiers with education, job skills, and fitting back into society. Save the Children's 2005 report "Forgotten Casualties of War: Girls in Armed Conflict" concludes that girls are caught between recrimination from the armed group if they leave and from the community if they return home and are invisible in reintegration programs. Misogyny and neglect on all sides has sent many of them into prostitution for survival or to take their lives. Former girls soldiers are more than twice as likely to commit suicide as boy counterparts.

The Fiction

For an exercise in irreality and moral depravity, Google *girl soldiers images*. You will find a garbage heap of pornographic images: cartoons of large-breasted, barely clothed women with big thighs and some muscles. They wield a gun in each hand and look like the sex industry's version of strippers and so-called happy hookers costumed for Armed Services Day. Sprinkled among them are photos of actual young women soldiers, hanging out passively like decorations among male soldiers. Of the first two hundred images I perused, only a handful portrayed real girl soldiers, serious beyond years with sad-to-death eyes. Yet even those photos lack the gruesome reality of the tens of thousands of girls entrapped in armies and militias.

For contrast, look at Google's *child soldiers images*. Ninety-five percent of child soldier images are boys. All are realistic war photos with children carrying, aiming, and shooting weapons sometimes longer than they are tall; roaming streets in search of prey; poised to kill, faces deadly serious, some hardened, some older than their years, others still bearing traces of their stolen childhood. No airbrushed or pornographic reality on that site. Only a crucial omission: real girl soldiers—who constitute up to forty percent of child soldiers and suffer the most vile sexual violation and rejection—are missing.

Actions Needed

Because using children, by whatever means, in armed conflict is an internationally recognized crime against humanity by the International Criminal Court, we must take action:

+ dedicate forty percent of funding available for the rehabilitation of child soldiers to the reintegration of girls within their communities
+ indict and prosecute leaders who use child soldiers
+ research countries that traffic in arms or whose businesses invest in or trade with countries using child soldiers, and
+ publicize, stigmatize, lobby, and boycott violators

We, in the United States, need a national floodlight on the issue of child soldiers to frame and shame the hypocrisy of passing a law to protect children caught in conflict and then violating it for that morbid excuse of "national security"—a coverall for American militarism, xenophobia, torture, erasure of civil rights, and sexual exploitation. Otherwise, political statements that *women's rights are human rights* are a sham.

Originally published October 20, 2016, at *Truthdig*. Reprinted with permission.

No Climate Justice without Justice for Women

I am looking at the faces of ten-year-old girls from across the world—faces brimming with expectancy. The 2016 UN report *The Face of the Future* opens with their photos and this introduction:

With support from family, community and nation, and the full realization of her rights, a ten-year-old girl can thrive and help bring about the future we all want.

What the world will look like in fifteen years will depend on our doing everything in our power to ignite the potential of the ten-year-old girl today.

What the world will look like in fifteen years depends also on our human commitment to reduce substantially greenhouse gas emissions and achieve at least fifty percent of energy from renewable sources by 2030 so that her world remains habitable. However, we cannot get to a sustainable world without full realization of girls' and women's rights, for women are responsible for providing food, fuel, and water for billions of people in much of Africa and Asia, where natural resources are growing scarce and rapidly degrading. Yet, many women there lack the right to own land or access credit and technical training to assure sustainability of their natural resources.

We will not get there in fifteen years without women's equality in decision-making because women in governance positions sign on to international treaties that take action against climate change more so than male counterparts. Further, there is abundant evidence that women care more about the environment than men and handle risk—economic, environmental, and personal—more wisely than men.

Climate change predictions worsen daily, while climate change victims only increase. Consider these findings by 2017:

- climate is changing 170 times faster due to human activity than through natural forces, and
- within 40 years, up to 1.5 billion people could be climate change migrants and refugees from rising seas

Worsening drought, deforestation, and desertification mean that women in developing countries must walk farther distances for fuel and water with higher risk of sexual violence, carry heavier loads, and work harder to grow enough food for their families. In one rural Sudanese community, the time required to gather fuelwood quadrupled over a decade. Heavier loads over longer distances cause spinal damage, pregnancy complications, and higher maternal mortality. Girls drop out of school more than boys to assist their mothers, thus setting girls up for less education and greater poverty than their brothers. Moreover, in times of crop scarcity, women will give priority of food to their husbands and sons.

In the early 1990s, solar cookers—a renewable technology that liberates women from firewood collection for income-earning activities and preserves carbon-sequestering biomass—were introduced in Zimbabwe. The project failed because men opposed women learning a technology that the men knew nothing about. Thus the mantra, *No climate justice without justice for women.*

Climate and Natural Disasters

Embedded within climate science and the study of those most vulnerable to climate change and natural disasters is a rarely acknowledged fact, namely, that women and girls are the paramount victims. The extent of that injustice and its roots lies in women's inequality. A multitude of discriminatory economic, cultural, and social factors converge to worsen climate-change impacts for women. Among them are greater female poverty, fewer resources, and less power in their society; physical limits imposed on women and girls; and increased sexual violence during and after climate-related disasters. All contribute to women's greater mortality, destitution, and sexual victimization during extreme climate events.

Though not a climate-related natural disaster, the 2004 Asian tsunami, which killed more than 220,000 people in twelve countries, caused an extreme excess of deaths among women and girls. It serves to shed light on social inequalities that undermine women's survival from climate-change disasters. During the tsunami, some women drowned because of being weighed down by their saris and others because they had never been taught to swim. Girls drowned because they had never learned to climb trees like their brothers. Many women died because they stayed behind to look for their children and other relatives. In one known case, a father struggling to hold his son and daughter from drowning let go of his daughter's hand because he considered his son more important, given he would carry on the family line.

Yet women's vulnerability in disasters rarely recedes with the floodwaters. Male violence against women increases with the chaos of natural and climate-related disasters just as it does with social breakdown in war and conflict.

Typhoon Haiyan

The Philippines, one of the most vulnerable countries to climate change and an epicenter of super typhoons, is a magnet for sex traffickers who prey on homeless victims after disasters. In the wake of the 2013 Typhoon Haiyan, the strongest typhoon ever recorded at the time, an underground economy sprang up in the City of Tacloban Astrodome where thousands of displaced Filipinos sought shelter. Girls and women were sold into prostitution for food and aid supplies. Others were offered jobs and scholarships but then trafficked to the Angeles City red-light district, a legacy of the former US Clark Air Force Base that operated for nearly a century. Nearly eighty percent of women and girls exploited in sex clubs and bars in Angeles City are from climate-change vulnerable areas. Climate change—a boon for traffickers, pimps, and johns—victimizes women and girls triply with the loss of home, livelihood, and heightened risk of sexual exploitation.

Hurricane Katrina

More than a quarter of African–American women in New Orleans were living in poverty when Hurricane Katrina struck the Gulf Coast in August 2005 with winds up to 140 miles per hour and storm surges that broke through barrier levees. Few had cars, and those who could escape were stranded around the city at heightened risk of sexual assault. Further, pregnancy and recent childbirth limited the mobility of some.

By 2008, the number of Black single mothers living in poverty had declined precipitously in New Orleans, their having been displaced by the government decision to raze public housing. Higher income whites replaced them as gentrification overran the city. They became climate migrants scattered across southern states. No studies to date have determined their fate.

"Thems that got will get, and thems that's not will lose," wrote Fatima Shalk of New Orleans, summing up the winner and losers of Katrina and the fate of the US poor in future climate-change disasters. The Union for Concerned Scientists reports that by 2035 more than half of US communities that will flood recurrently and disruptively are low-income with predominantly residents of color.

In the year after Hurricane Katrina, in neighboring storm-battered Mississippi, violence against women increased four-fold. Two years later, the rate was more than double.

Investing in Women

Gender formally entered UN deliberations on climate change only in 2008, more than two decades after climate studies and conferences were launched by the UN. Subsequent studies and women's testimonies have exposed the layers of climate impacts on women, worsened by gender-based inequality in their societies, and the studies and testimonies also provide compelling evidence to invest in women as agents of land, water, and forest restoration.

Greenbelt Movement

In the 1970s, Wangari Maathai, the first East African woman to receive a PhD, set off a revolution to rejuvenate the deforested and desertifying environment of Kenya, her home country. Partnering with women's groups, she initiated community-based tree-planting efforts in what became the Greenbelt Movement and that spread to dozens of other countries. Forty years later, more than forty million trees had transformed landscapes as well as the lives and minds of women with whom Maathai worked. The skills, knowledge, and income they gained, as she testified, brought self-confidence and independence. Given women's relationship to forests in developing countries, it is no surprise that a study of deforestation in sixty-one countries between 1990 and 2005 found that countries with numerous and large women's and environmental non-governmental organizations had significantly lower levels of forest loss.

Andra Pradesh

Agriculture contributes at least a quarter of India's greenhouse gas emissions, nitrous oxide from fertilizers being one of the sources. More than five thousand women in seventy-five villages of the arid interior of the state of Andra Pradesh offer an exemplary mitigating alternative. Working with women's village associations called Sanghams, the Deccan Development Society has facilitated their transition to income-generating organic agriculture using indigenous crops that need less water, restoring medicinal plants, and reclaiming degraded land by planting neighborhood forests—more than one million trees—over twenty-five years. Their companion accomplishments include a seed bank and loan system for women farmers, a community radio station that reaches two hundred villages, and production of videos on methods of organic agriculture, seed saving, and the hazards of genetic engineering in agriculture.

Most are Dalits, the broken, the poorest of the poor in India's rigid caste system. The story of one, Chinna Narsamma the Radio Jockey, mirrors the transformation of both their environment and themselves achieved by many thousands of heretofore-impoverished castaways of society. Narsamma, who never had formal education, now "womans" a radio station, produces films, speaks in-country and abroad about the Andra Pradesh model, and also cultivates her own twenty acres of organic agriculture. In a region challenged with barren land, semi-arid conditions, and frequent droughts, women farmers have been able to banish hunger and provide an exemplary model of climate justice with justice for women.

Woman-Centered Policy and Actions

The best projects tackle environmental problems while markedly improving the lives of women and girls.

—Monique Barbut, executive secretary
UN Convention to Combat Desertification

The following recommendations, gleaned from pilot projects and successful programs, are the tip of the iceberg regarding the potential for women's contribution to mitigating and adapting to climate change as well as to their own liberation simultaneously:

- train women technicians in water-saving and solar technologies
- hire female as well as male trainers to teach climate-adaptation farming
- draw from women's indigenous knowledge about seeds, soil, and natural resources
- recruit women for emergency planning, especially emergency evacuation methods and routes to ensure women can escape during climate disasters
- assure fair and non-discriminatory allocation of disaster relief resources, including food, housing, and clothing, and

- include women in local and regional decision-making councils and increase women's leadership in delegations to the UN climate accord conferences

All of those prescriptions and many more presume that *empowering women*–through access to credit and technical training, through land ownership and equal economic and political decision-making roles–is key to mitigating and adapting to climate change in both developing and developed countries.

Correspondingly, all of the recommendations–if they are to materialize–oblige men to share power with women and to commit to eliminating social, legal, and cultural discrimination against women as well as all forms of violence against women—in other words, a sea change in the patriarchal order of things.

The World Bank reported in 2015 that of 173 economies studied, nine in ten had at least one law impeding women's economic empowerment, including access to credit. As I write in 2017, the allegedly democratic United States has a meager nineteen percent of women in Congress, and a majority of US men polled do not want a female president in their lifetimes. As for the ten major US environmental NGOs, eighty percent are run by white men, though polls suggest that women, Native Americans, Latinos, African Americans, and Asians care more and are more seriously affected by climate change.

If today's ten-year-old girls are to *thrive and help bring about a future we all want*, men need to cede their grip on power and women need to take power as partners in the project of transforming the governing paradigms of power. Otherwise, we are all doomed to men's Armageddons of climate change, nuclear weapons, war without end, extremes of inequality, and every form of sexualized and racialized violence.

May the UN Conventions on Climate Change and the Eradication of All Forms of Discrimination Against Women convene under the canopy of Climate Justice with Justice for Women.

Originally published August 30, 2017 at *Truthdig*. Reprinted with permission.

Biology Is Not Destiny

The Second Sex, a two-volume 1949 classic by French writer Simone de Beauvoir, quickly became an eminent—some contend the preeminent—book in the pantheon of twentieth-century feminist and existentialist writings. Like the biologist Rachel Carson's 1962 *Silent Spring*, *The Second Sex* kindled a revolution across the western world ablaze today in the global quest for women's human rights, as witnessed by the January 2017 Women's March on every continent, including Antarctica. De Beauvoir's core proposition animates every page: the subordination and inequality of women is not our fate by reason of our biology. It is a gendered construct of society that has been accepted as natural by most men and women for millennia.

Like a sower scattering seeds, de Beauvoir planted an abundance of critical thinking that fed the feminist revolution in consciousness and activism of the 1960s and 1970s—popularly known as the second wave of feminism. As with all radical social movements, debates and challenges ensued and persist. But the iconic message irrevocably lives: biology is not destiny. The reduction of women to the feminine, sexualized lesser sex is an artifice constructed of vested prejudices that deprive women and the world of our fullest existence.

A small book of selected extracts from *The Second Sex* was released under the title, *The Independent Woman*. It offers a trail studded with gems of insight, from which I cull a few to comment on today's events, findings, and social thinking regarding girls and women. Entwined within the extracts are a radical timelessness of feminist analysis and also the shortcomings of a period piece.

"Humanity is male," writes de Beauvoir, "and man defines woman not in herself, but in relation to himself: she is not considered an autonomous being. The male sex sees her essentially as a sexed being. He is a subject, She is the other." Here, however, de Beauvoir is not referring explicitly to widespread sexual violence against women, including stalking, sexual harassment, rape, pimping, exploitation of women in prostitution, lack of reproductive freedom, and other violations of women's bodies, psyches, and souls. Rather she signifies the condition of women: essentialized since birth into domestic and passive feminine roles and, as her contemporary Virginia Woolf writes in *A Room of One's Own*, serving "all these centuries as looking glasses possessing the magic and delicious power of reflecting the figure of man at twice its natural size."

De Beauvoir then describes the tangled web where women, unlike any other oppressed group, live intimately with their oppressors and often collude in their own oppression. "They live dispersed among men, tied by homes, work, economic interests and social conditions to certain men—fathers and husbands—more closely than to other women," writes de Beauvoir. She describes with great nuance the detritus of inequality among intimates, banalized in popular culture as the "battle between the sexes."

Her prescription for liberation and equality is straightforward: do what self-realized men have done. Seek a comparable education and aspire to excel. Set high goals for yourself in work and career. Don't fall prey to self-limiting messages from home, school, the workplace, society, and your own internalized version of sex-based inferiority— stellar messages to girls and women, but are they sufficient?

A 2018 nationally representative poll of one thousand US children and adolescents from ten to nineteen years old reveals that, while many girls and young women have sought and achieved substantial gains in precisely those prescriptions for achieving fulfill-ment, a riptide of sexual objectification persists as if to undermine their pursuit of equality and excellence.

"For me," responded thirteen-year-old Hiree Felema, "it's important to be intelligent and confident. For women, in society, I think people just want you to be attractive"—an insight echoed by many girls surveyed. Girls reported as much interest in math and science as boys and slightly more in leadership, yet they did not feel equal with respect to their bodies. Three quarters of teenage girls felt judged for their looks and unsafe as females, including from sexual predators online. Many reported boys asking for nude photos, daily hearing sexual comments or jokes from boys in school and from men in their families. And, interestingly, girls felt more pressure to be kind than boys did, reflecting society's stubborn, sex-based stereotypes of what is valued in women but not necessarily in men.

In 2017, the Pew Charitable Trust surveyed 4,573 Americans about what society values and—and doesn't—in men and women. *Power, leadership,* and *honesty* were positive attributes in men, whereas, *power* and *ambition* were largely seen as negative in women. *Compassionate, kind,* and *responsible* were qualities viewed positively for women, while *emotion* and *compassion* largely ranked negatively for men. Just half of respondents chose *independence* in women and *caring* in men as positive traits. Beauty was valued for women, but *provider* exclusively for men. Two hopeful results among the otherwise timeworn gender-based stereotypes: *brain* was valued in women and *sexism* negatively in men.

In the confirmation hearings of then-Supreme Court nominee Brett Kavanaugh, we had a riveting view of the outfall of privilege for entitled men who pander in unrestrained displays of anger, self-righteousness, and ambition. Had Dr. Christine Blasey Ford "spoken with the same tone and flippancy as Kavanaugh, she would have been described as unstable or combative," notes former Republican governor of New Jersey Christine Todd Whitman. Whitman's prescription? Increase the number of women in leadership roles, something white, married conservative women—identifying more with white men than other women—appear reluctant to do, judging from their voting patterns.

Since *The Second Sex,* the ascendancy of women has proven to be both more challenging than just imitating successful, "autonomous" men, as even aspiring eleven- and twelve-year-old girls know, and more complex than de Beauvoir proposed. Recent studies of women in leadership in public and private sectors have concluded that women in high-level positions and on boards deal more effectively with risk, focus more strategically on long-term priorities, and are more successful financially. Experimental studies of women and men negotiating post-conflict agreements have found that all male groups take riskier, less empathetic, and more aggressive positions. Their negotiations break down more quickly than those that include women. Further, men are more satisfied with decisions made when women are involved than with all-male groups.

Parsing those findings, many women, educated like men and in comparable positions of influence, integrate qualities of their socialized development—compassion, not acting rashly or aggressively, a sense of responsibility— as assets into their leadership. In other words, they set more integrated, smart, and nuanced goals for themselves than merely imitating men and have succeeded where men have not.

The lesson, insufficiently probed in *The Second Sex* as reflected in *The Independent Woman*, is that men need to work as hard and as persistently for their liberation from masculinism, especially the normative sexual objectification of women, as women have strived for our equality. As the Buddhist critic and teacher Lama Rod Owens states, "Like white people challenging whiteness, it is men who must do the work of understanding that a significant portion of our identity is based on a toxic, patriarchal masculinity. We need a widespread divestment in patriarchy and a complete interrogation of the ethics of power. We all have work to do."

Reaching our full human capacity is the task of both sexes. If that were achieved, the world—riven with wars, endangered by nuclear weapons and climate change, rent by increasing economic inequality and declining democracy, *under almost exclusive male leadership*—will have a far better chance of survival.

Men their rights and nothing more: Women their rights and nothing less.

—Susan B. Anthony, 1868

Originally published March 8, 2019 at *Truthdig*. Reprinted with permission.

Hope

an afterword by Pat Hynes

We live in a time of diminishing hope with worsening climate crisis and insufficient will among those most responsible—major industrial countries—to radically reduce their emissions now, not a decade or three decades from now. We cohabitate with more than thirteen thousand nuclear weapons spread among hostile nations, and many of those weapons are now being upgraded, thus raising the already very high risk of nuclear apocalypse. The Pentagon is predicting, planning, and pursuing, it appears, war with China and Russia in the Indo-Pacific, the Arctic, and in space.

Since the COVID pandemic began, extremes between the haves and have-nots have widened, making the United States the most unequal of any society at any time in history, according to French economist Thomas Piketty. Wealthy nations have hoarded COVID-19 vaccine, inoculating at twenty-five times the rate of poorer countries as of April 2021. By late May, more than seventy-five percent of all vaccines were administered in only ten countries. Likewise, ongoing sexual and racial exploitation of women and girls—the most common but least punished crime in the world—worsened during COVID, according to the United Nations.

In the midst of such dystopian trends, experts who study existential threats have concluded that the chance of human extinction is higher than at any time in human history, some three hundred thousand years. Without even knowing the "experts'" conclusion, many of us have had to examine our sense of hope and where we experience it. For what we choose in the face of diminishing prospects for our world—action, despair, or some place in between—will determine how fully, how resolutely we live.

Hope upwells in me now in smaller places and actions, no matter their chance of success—when I witness, for example, the countless bold and creative actions undertaken by youth across the world on behalf of their future; by victim survivors resisting their oppression; by a small prescient group challenging the majority consensus; and by an unexpected outcome defying the naysayers.

The Few Prescient vs. the Majority Consensus

In 2011, President Barack Obama proclaimed a "Pivot to Asia" that in time was recognized as a process of building a coalition of Indo-Pacific partners for a new Cold War with China, portrayed as a growing threat to US economic dominance and challenge to US military hegemony. The chorus of Pentagon voices since has risen to a hawkish crescendo: "China is using 'pernicious' behavior to challenge US dominance in the region (i.e., in China's neighborhood) and to remake the international order in its image," that is, to replace our image, remarked former US Indo-Pacific commander, Admiral Philip Davidson.

"China aims to displace the US as the world's pre-eminent superpower," according to Avril Haines, director of national intelligence, in her recent assessment of key threats facing the United States.

"Our pacing threat is the Chinese," asserted Army General James Dickinson, US Space Command director, while meeting with Japanese counterparts. Embodying an unparalleled human hubris, his area of operations is outer space, that is 62 miles above the earth to infinity. Containing China by whatever means necessary is the reason for a proposal from President Joseph R. Biden for a 1.7% increase in the Pentagon budget for fiscal year 2022.

Enter Pivot to Peace

Pivot to Peace states,

We are concerned Americans from all walks of life—military veterans, public sector workers, healthcare professionals, and more—who have come together in opposition to the dramatically increasing drive toward confrontation between the United States and China.

We have launched a new effort to educate and mobilize public opinion about the benefits of a policy that facilitates cooperation and mutual respect between the United States and China. We believe that friendship and engagement between our countries is the better path towards the future.

Youth Defining Their Future

Oil companies, among the largest and most powerful companies in history, have controlled the destiny of some countries and served as the taproot of many wars since the 1970s, undermining democracy. Their enterprise constitutes the single greatest factor in our climate crisis. The industry enjoys a reliable revolving door between itself and government, where it gains undue power over energy legislation and policy. Massive government subsidies—much larger proportionally than for solar and wind—enable oil companies to stay profitable and forestall a renewable energy revolution. Further, fossil fuel companies comprise the top ten corporations that have invested the most money since 2017 lobbying for anti-protest bills, that is, bills to punish citizen protestors.

Enter Voices of Sanity

"I believe a better world is possible," declares seventeen-year-old Chanté Davis, a climate refugee and activist, who continues,

> I've lived through too many climate disasters to count. When I was two years old, my family fled our home in New Orleans as Hurricane Katrina came barreling into the Gulf Coast. After moving to Houston, Hurricane Harvey flooded my home and shattered any hope of normalcy. And just this year, my family and friends struggled to stay warm as the Texas freeze wiped out power for millions across the state.

With other young Sunrise Movement activists, Davis began a four-hundred-mile Generation-on-Fire march in mid-May 2021 for a better Green New Deal across the Gulf South from New Orleans to Houston. She explained,

> We are marching to push Biden to take big, bold action to stop this climate crisis following in the footsteps of Black, brown, and indigenous people who have been leading the fight here for centuries.

Defying the Naysayers

We can barely read the words immigrant and refugee without their being conjoined with crisis. Most wealthy countries in Western Europe and the United States have closed their doors to people fleeing poverty, violence, corruption, and climate crisis—often people from regions they formerly colonized, always people from lower-income countries. In fact, countries receiving most refugees—Lebanon, Jordan, Turkey, Liberia, and Uganda—are not high-income countries. The two wealthy exceptions are industrialized Germany and Sweden.

Refugees Welcome

In 2015 and 2016, the government of Angela Merkel welcomed more than a million refugees from the Middle East and North Africa. What was deemed an "immigrant crisis" at the time, fought by a resurgent German extreme right and forecast to bring Merkel down, has been a notable success. Immigrants are indispensable among an aging German population, and, with training and internships, they are rapidly integrating into the labor market. At the same time, Germany has sustained the strongest economy in Europe and defied predictions of chaos: the far right has ebbed, the Green Party has surged, and Merkel sustained her leadership.

Survivor Leaders

Human trafficking for sexual exploitation is global—in every town, city, and country of the world. The majority of its victims are women and girls, overwhelmingly women and girls of color within the most disadvantaged groups in their societies. In the United States, according to the Coalition on Trafficking in Women, Black women and girls are more likely to be sex trafficked, sexually violated, and exploited while being criminalized for their exploitation by state law and law enforcement.

Enter the Emma Coalition

Survivors-of-prostitution who have founded exit programs for women and girls in prostitution and have partnered with advocates and organizations lead the Equality Model in Massachusetts, EMMA, Coalition. In their words, "we can make our state a leader in the fight against this most exploitative practice, especially against our most vulnerable populations." A major feature of their activism is advocating on behalf of legislation, an act to Strengthen Justice and Support for Sex Trade Survivors.

Key provisions of the legislation would achieve:

- decriminalizing those bought and sold for sexual exploitation and expunging all past charges of prostitution
- penalizing the crime of buying sex with an income-based fine and redirecting fines to support survivor-led programs throughout the state, and
- creating an interagency committee to augment opportunities for health, mental health, housing, job training, employment, and education for prostituted persons

The medieval theologian Thomas Aquinas observed that hope requires "friends to rely on"–companions on our quest like Chante Davis marching with other youth who, like her, believe another world is possible. Vaclav Havel, first president of the Czech Republic, noted that "Hope is not the same as joy that things are going well or headed for early success, but rather an ability to work for something *because it is good*," such as friendship and engagement between the US and China.

A singular, affirmative arc of history against a larger adverse trend gives hope, such as enabling a million refugees to live a freer, fuller life, among the many millions denied it and empowering hundreds of women and girls in Massachusetts, among the many millions across the world exploited in prostitution, to leave it.

We create conditions for hope when we aspire to something both good and badly needed and when we work toward achieving it, no matter the odds. And, if enough of humanity joins in this, we can improve the odds of human survival.

Originally published June 8, 2021 in *Portside*. Reprinted with permission.

Sources and Recommended Resources

Climate Crisis

Climate News Network ◆ climatenewsnetwork.net

Inside Climate News, newsletters@insideclimatenews.org

IPCC 2021 Summary Report ◆ ipcc.ch/report/ar6/wg1
   downloads/report/IPCC_AR6_WGI_SPM.pdf

Union of Concerned Scientists ◆ ucsusa.org

Domestic and Foreign Policy

Common Dreams ◆ commondreams.org

Fairness and Accuracy in Reporting
   fairnessandaccuracyinreporting.org

Foreign Policy in Focus ◆ fpif.org

Inequality.org

Informed Comment ◆ juancole.com

Institute for Policy Studies ◆ ips-dc.org

In These Times ◆ inthesetimes.com

The Nation ◆ thenation.com

Politico ◆ politico.com

Portside ◆ portside.org

ProPublica ◆ propublica.org

Scheerpost ◆ scheerpost.com

Truthdig ◆ truthdig.com

Truthout ◆ truthout.org

Feminism

Coalition Against Trafficking in Women
catwinternational.org

Feminist Foreign Policy ◆ centreforfeministforeignpolicy.org

Institute for Women's Policy Research ◆ iwpr.org

Progress of the World's Women
unwomen.org

Women's International League for Peace and Freedom, WILPF
wilpf.org

WUNRN ◆ wunrn.com

Media

Democracy Now ◆ democracynow.org

Military and Militarism

Brown University Costs of War Project
watson.brown.edu/costsofwar/

DOD, E-News ◆ defensenews.com

Military Times ◆ militarytimes.org

Tom Dispatch ◆ TomDispatch.com

World Beyond War ◆ worldbeyondwar.org

Nuclear Power and Weapons

Beyond Nuclear ◆ beyondnuclearinternational.org

Bulletin of the Atomic Scientists ◆ newsletter@thebulletin.org

ICAN ◆ nuclearban.us/ican-the-international-campaign-to
abolish-nuclear-weapons/Nuclear Ban.us nuclearban.us

NIRS ◆ nirs.org

Peace

CodePink ◆ codepink.org

Massachusetts Peace Action ◆ masspeaceaction.org

Women Against War ◆ womenagainstwar.org/wordpress/

World Beyond War ◆ worldbeyondwar.org

Women's International League for Peace and Freedom ◆ wilpf.org

Racial Justice

Black Lives Matter ✦ blacklivesmatter.com

Black Past ✦ blackpast.org

GLAD Racial Justice Resources ✦ glad.org/racial-justice
resources/

Renewable Energy and Efficiency

Rocky Mountain Institute ✦ rmi.org

Stanford University ✦ energystanford.edu

Union of Concerned Scientists ✦ ucs.usa

Veterans

Iraq Veterans Against the War ✦ ivaw.org

Organization of Women's Freedom in Iraq ✦ owfi.info/EN/

Service Women's Action Network ✦ servicewomen.org

Veterans for Peace ✦ veteransforpeace.org

Books on Topics Related to Hope and Justice

Breyman, Steve, Amidon, John W., Baillargeon Aumand, Maureen, eds. *Bending the Arc: Striving for Peace and Justice in an Age of Endless War.* Albany: SUNY Press, 2020.

Chappell, Paul K. *Soldiers of Peace: How to Wield the Weapon of Nonviolence with Maximum Force.* Westport and New York: Prospecta Press, 2017.

Frank, Dana. *The Long Honduran Night: Resistance, Terror, and the United States in the Aftermath of the Coup.* Chicago: Haymarket Books, 2018.

Fry, Douglas P. *The Human Potential for Peace: An Anthropological Challenge to Assumptions about War and Violence.* New York and Oxford: Oxford University Press, 2006.

Gbowee, Leymah with Mithers, Carol. *Mighty Be Our Powers: How Sisterhood, Prayer, and Sex Changed a Nation at War.* New York: Beast Books, 2011.

Gonzalez, Juan. *Harvest of Empire: A History of Latinos in America.* London: Penguin Books, 2011.

Grossman, Lieutenant Colonel Dave. *On Killing: The Psychological Cost of Learning to Kill in War and Society.* Boston: Little Brown and Company, 1995.

Books on Topics Related to Hope and Justice
continued

Harjo, Joy. *An American Sunrise.* New York: W.W. Norton & Co., 2019.

Hauter, Wenonah. *Frackopoly: The Battle for the Future of Energy and the Environment.* New York: The New Press, 2016.

Jamail, Dahr. *The End of Ice: Bearing Witness and Finding Meaning in the Path of Climate Disruption.* New York: The New Press, 2019.

Johnson, Ayana Elizabeth and Katharine K. Wilkinson. eds. *All We Can Save: Truth, Courage, and Solutions for the Climate Crisis.* New York: One World, 2020.

Johnson, Chalmers. *Dismantling the Empire: America's Last Best Hope.* New York: Metropolitan Books, Henry Holt and Company, 2010.

Johnson, Chalmers. *The Sorrows of Empire: Militarism, Secrecy, and the End of the Republic.* New York: Metropolitan Books, Henry Holt and Company, 2004.

Jones, Ann. *War Is Not Over When It's Over: Women Speak Out From the Ruins of War.* New York: Metropolitan Books, Henry Holt and Company, 2010.

Kinzer, Stephen. *Overthrow: America's Century of Regime Change from Hawaii to Iraq.* New York: Times Books, Henry Holt and Company, 2006.

Kinzer, Stephen. *The True Flag: Theodore, Mark Twain, and the Birth of the American Empire.* New York: St. Martin's Press, 2017.

Klein, Naomi. *No Is Not Enough: Resisting Trump's Shock Politics and Winning the World We Need.* Chicago: Haymarket Books, 2017.

McDonnell, Faith J. and Akallo, Grace. *Girlsoldier: A Story of Hope for Northern Uganda's Children.* Grand Rapids, Michigan: Chosen, 2007.

Perlman, Wendy. *We Crossed a Bridge and It Trembled. Voices from Syria.* New York: HarperCollins Publishers, 2017.

Vine, David. *Base Nation: How U.S. Military Bases Abroad Harm America and the World.* New York: Metropolitan Books, Henry Holt and Company, 2015.

Zinn, Howard. *The Bomb.* San Francisco: City Lights Books, 2010.

Acknowledgements

My deepest thanks to all who, across a lifetime, taught me to think critically, especially feminists, and to those from whom I learned and continue to learn empathy, love, friendship, sisterhood, and a sense of community by your example and your gifts of those to me.

My loving, enduring thanks to my sisters and brothers: we are a tightly woven web in the spirit our parents hoped for us. With solid support, you have read most of the articles included in *HOPE, BUT DEMAND JUSTICE*. And to the many readers who have written to me and encouraged more writing, your affirmation has propelled me forward.

Thank you, my companions in western Massachusetts in mutual commitment to peace, social justice, and sustaining life on Earth, especially Traprock Center for Peace and Justice board and also the Interfaith Council of Franklin County, FC CPR Peace Task Force, Nuclear Free Future, the Resistance Center, Climate Action Now, the Wendell State Forest Alliance, Greening Greenfield, Racial Justice Rising, Jewish Activists for Immigration Justice of Western Massachusetts, Pioneer Valley Interfaith Refugee Action Group, CodePink Western Massachusetts, and the community standing out each Saturday morning on the Greenfield Common. More widely, thank you to Massachusetts Peace Alliance, Women's International League for Peace and Freedom, especially Nancy Price and Marguerite Adelman; peace groups across the country who have invited me to give in-person talks and webinars; and my feminist, environmental, and peace partners in Sierra Leone, especially

Kadie Sesay and Pastor Peter Alfred; in Cameroon, especially Guy Feugap; and in Vietnam, especially Phung Tuu Boi, and in many other corners of the world. For all who helped in fundraising for Vietnam projects and donated generously to scholarships for Agent Orange-injured children and 10,000 Trees for Vietnam, especially Diana Roberts, Andy Rothschild, Nancy Hazard, and Alice Swift with Mount Toby Quakers, your gifts continue to give.

Dr. Evelyn Murphy, your always honest, astute comments on my articles in HOPE, BUT DEMAND JUSTICE and your own most accomplished life and feminist sisterhood have been fuel that recharges my political convictions.

Randy Kehler and the late Doris Bunte, each large in respect, goodness, and political impact, how fortunate I am to have had you as companions on the journey.

My publisher, Marcia Gagliardi, suggested the book that became HOPE, BUT DEMAND JUSTICE and has hovered over it like a guardian angel with a penchant for meticulous detail—mille grazie. And to the editors at Truthdig, Truthout, Common Dreams, Portside, ZCommunications, Informed Comment, and Peace and Freedom, the Greenfield Recorder, and the many regional newspapers, what would I have done without your welcoming forums?

My dear, singular sister Margaret, how fortunate I am to have had your astute early reading of numerous articles in HOPE, BUT DEMAND JUSTICE. Eileen Barrett and Darcy Sweeney, thank you for your lucid reading, suggested edits and, more so, your abiding friendship.

And final, infinite thanks to the Earth—animal, vegetable, and mineral—you give me life, inspiration, and meaning.

The book title HOPE, BUT DEMAND JUSTICE was inspired by a wall hanging of that title made by Lesyslie Rackard, a member of Sisters in Stitches Joined in the Cloth. With her generous permission to use her title, she offered the following:

> We marched, demonstrated, held rallies, and sang for peace.
> All social movements in the name of justice and peace have been happening for more than four hundred years, but not until 2020 have we had a digital awakening in the middle of a COVID-19

pandemic. It was a spotlight on the State-sanctioned violence and crimes against people of color within our neighborhoods and communities. My wall-hanging "HOPE, BUT DEMAND JUSTICE" is inspired by my grandchildren, great-nieces, and all the young activists who stood on the corners and marched in my community and chanted "Black lives matter." It is my hope it will bring about the changes needed for our future generations.

Pat Hynes
photo by Paul Franz
courtesy of the *Greenfield Recorder*

About the Author

Pat Hynes, formally known as H. Patricia Hynes, is a retired environmental engineer who worked as a Superfund engineer for EPA New England and as a professor of Environmental Health on multi-racial and low-income issues of the urban environment, including lead poisoning, asthma, and the indoor environment in public housing, community gardens, and urban agriculture; environmental justice; and feminism at Boston University School of Public Health.

For her Superfund work and her writing, teaching, and community-based research projects at Boston University, she has won national, regional, and local awards from US EPA, American Public Health Association, Boston University School of Public Health, Massachusetts Commission of Conservation Commissions, Boston Natural Areas Network, and her alma maters Chestnut Hill College and the University of Massachusetts Amherst.

She is the author and editor of seven books, including *The Recurring Silent Spring*, nominated for the Gustavus Myers Outstanding Book Award. She won the 1996 National Arbor Day Foundation Book Award for *A Patch of Eden*, her book on community gardens in inner cities.

Pat writes and speaks on the health effects of war and militarism on society and, in particular, on women. She also writes about climate justice, renewable energy, and hazards of nuclear weapons. As former director from 2010 to 2020 and then board member of Traprock Center for Peace and Justice in western Massachusetts, she is committed to building the Traprock Center as a collaborative educational and project-based center in peace and justice leadership for activists, educators, and students.

She has written many articles on nuclear power and nuclear weapons, climate change, war and militarism, peace and the effects of war on women and the environment published nationally and internationally in journals, books, newspapers, and online.

Pat Hynes conducted an investigation in 2014 of the ongoing legacy of Agent Orange in Vietnam and created the Vietnam Peace Village Project to support scholarships for third- and fourth-generation Agent Orange victims and also 10,000 Trees for Vietnam: an Environmental Justice Collaboration to support tree planting in areas de-forested by Agent Orange.

Since 2018, she has sustained a partnership with the Women's International League for Peace and Freedom, WILPF, Sierra Leone branch that includes providing children's books on peace, social justice, and environment for their use in schools and computer supplies for WILPF Sierra Leone's new office to help launch their countrywide work; a Sports for Peace initiative with youth; a COVID-19 education effort; and the Respect for Girls program. With WILPF US, she is co-developing a framework for Feminist Foreign Policy.

Colophon

Text and captions for *HOPE, BUT DEMAND JUSTICE* are set in Adobe Jenson, an old-style serif typeface drawn for Adobe Systems by its chief type designer Robert Slimbach. Its Roman styles are based on a text face cut by Nicolas Jenson in Venice around 1470, and its italics are based on those created by Ludovico Vicentino degli Arrighi fifty years later.

Jenson is an organic design with a low x-height. It is considered a highly readable typeface and is accordingly often used in book design for body text.

Titles for *HOPE, BUT DEMAND JUSTICE* are set in Franklin Gothic from a large family of sans-serif typefaces in the industrial or grotesque style developed in the early years of the twentieth century by the type foundry American Type Founders and credited to its head designer Morris Fuller Benton. Gothic was a contemporary term now little-used except to describe period designs meaning sans-serif.

Franklin Gothic has been used in many advertisements and headlines in newspapers. The typeface continues to maintain a high profile, appearing in a variety of media from books to billboards. Despite a period of eclipse in the 1930s after the introduction of European faces like Kabel and Futura, Franklin Gothic was rediscovered by American designers in the 1940s and has remained popular.

Benton's Franklin Gothic family is a set of solid designs, particularly suitable for display and trade use such as headlines rather than for extended text. Many versions and adaptations have been made since.

CPSIA information can be obtained
at www.ICGtesting.com
Printed in the USA
JSHW031008110622
26959JS00007B/215

9 781948 380553